Flowers from Fabrics

By the same author
Flowers From Feathers

Flowers from Fabrics

Pamela Woods

David & Charles
Newton Abbot   London
Vancouver

ISBN 0 7153 7254 8

Photoset in 12 on 13 pt Bembo
and printed in Great Britain by
Redwood Burn Limited
Trowbridge & Esher
for David & Charles (Publishers) Limited
Brunel House Newton Abbot Devon

Published in Canada
by Douglas David & Charles Limited
1875 Welch Street North Vancouver BC

Contents

Introduction

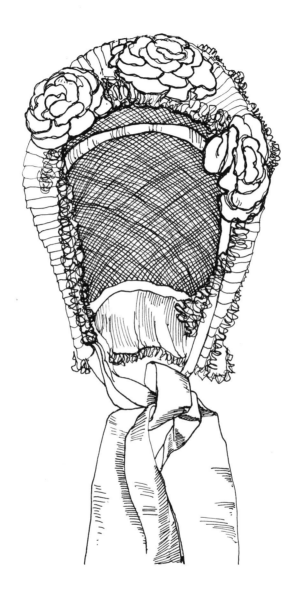

This beautiful Victorian child's bonnet was given to me by a friend whose great-aunt had left it in a suitcase. Trimmed with lace and ribbon, three delicate fabric flowers decorate the front.

1 Straw hat, 1747

Flowers, delicate objects of exquisite beauty, have been for ages and still are a constant source of inspiration for craftsmen and designers. Architects have chosen them to decorate their buildings, artists to fill their pictures, and fashion designers to incorporate in or adorn their creations. Glass and china designers, jewellery makers, silversmiths, blacksmiths, cabinet makers, sculptors and calligraphers use them too – the list is endless – but it is the connection of fashion with the art of floral decoration with which we are primarily concerned.

Floral designs stitched, woven or painted onto fabric are an accepted form of decoration, but here we seek to develop three-dimensional flowers made from the pieces of fabric remaining after dressmaking. What better way to complete an ensemble than to wear a flower made from your dress remnants in your hat. This fashion accessory used to hold prominent position in ladies' wardrobes in the eighteenth and nineteenth centuries. Hats were generally large to protect elaborate hairstyles from the elements and so provided an excellent place for floral decoration. The flat straw hat made in 1747 (Fig 1) is virtually a shelf on which the flowers are lying. It seems that the size of a

2 Fashion plates from *La Belle Assemblée 1827*

hat at this time in no way limited the number of flowers piled upon it; see the 1827 examples illustrated (Fig 2) and imagine the effort required to balance all that on their heads. Sometimes the flowers were even combined with feathers and ribbons as well.

Flowers nestling beside a lady's face, whether in her hair or under her bonnet, can be charming as are the bunches of flowers in the illustration of a bonnet made in 1856 (Fig 3).

Fabrics like silk, velvet and organdie were often used for flowers. It is interesting to see how the Italians made use of straw, their favourite material, for this hat made in 1750 (Fig 4), an example of the art of flower making used to perfection. The flower design round the brim is echoed in the three-dimensional flowers round the crown. It is a pity that more examples have not survived of objects which played such a prominent part in fashion. It is always sad to see a bloom wilting; obviously the fabric flowers had hard wear and one can understand how easily they became damaged, as shown by their use on the evening dress of 1879 (Fig 5). The very high hairstyles were in themselves an excellent place for flowers. We are now accustomed to seeing flowers from head to toe.

3 A bonnet, 1856

4 Italian straw hat, 1750

5 Evening dress, 1879

By 1900 it was the fashion to wear large straw hats with wide brims to stroll in the garden, protected from the sun. The brims were large enough to happily support cabbage roses all round (Fig 6). Twenty years later fashion lines became severe and simple with no fuss or frills save only for the corsage as we know it today. Usually worn on the shoulder these flowers were extremely large, but fashion allowed this. Now, as is often the case, we have turned full circle and it is considered fashionable to wear a flower as dress decoration. Those ingenious Victorian craftswomen seemed to have endless patience. Their inventiveness is unrivalled owing to their constant attention to detail and the possibilities of the materials they were using. This glass dome is quite incredible as every single flower and leaf is made with wool, either knotted, woven or sewn together (Fig 7).

Rather than be discouraged by their ability, you should feel inspired to try making some flowers of your own. Absorb all the information you can from artificial and real flowers and then, with the use of some of the modern materials available, see what fantasy flowers you can make.

6 Hat with roses worn by Miss Heather Firbank, 1909

7 All the flowers under this Victorian glass dome are made in various intriguing ways from interwoven wool. Combined with coral and fabric leaves, the maker's patience and handiwork has been perfectly preserved.

Before you start

Flowers made with fabrics are fantasy flowers which, by their structure, composed of a seed on a stem with petals round it, are accepted as flowers. They are bound to vary enormously, from those closely resembling real flowers to those which are purely imaginary. I am constantly interested in real flowers of all kinds, but view them with the possibility of reconstructing them from some form of material. One can never improve on nature but close imitations can be made. If a copy of a real flower becomes too complicated, that is the moment to simplify the flower to allow the quality of the material to show. Often it is the simple flowers that are delicately beautiful rather than over-complicated ones.

To make flowers for a balanced and varied combination, a contrast in shapes is an essential requirement. So many hand-made flowers tend to be round shapes, so try to include some long spikes, some leaves and also some profile flowers, those which face sideways and can also hang downwards if necessary.

Before you start any flower you should make a tight hook on the top of a stem wire and join the binding wire you intend to use (Fig 8). Test the strength of the join; this may seem unnecessary but it can be very disappointing if, after considerable effort in constructing your flower, the head comes off.

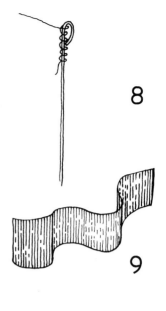

However simple or elaborate a flower, it will, unless formed around a plant seedhead on an existing stem, require a wire stem and some form of binding tape. This can be one of the plastic tapes made especially for the purpose like gutta percha or stem bind. If these are unavailable, thin strips of crepe paper or crepe fabric would make adequate substitutes. These last two materials may be more suitable to you because of the large range of colours available as opposed to the conventional stem binds which are only greens, browns or white. You should ensure that, whichever form of crepe you use, the crinkles run across the width of the strip so that when the stem is bound the strip will be held in place by tension (Fig 9). A little glue applied to the beginning and end of the crepe binding will prevent it from working loose. Another point to remember is to ensure that you cover the base of the petals very thoroughly; failure to do so will not only spoil the flower but will require a second binding which will result in a clumsy stem covering.

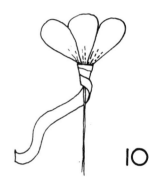

To cover a stem start by binding the base of the petals thoroughly (Fig 10) then, holding the stem with your thumb and forefinger, hold the tape still with the other hand and rotate the stem and the binding will form a spiral during the rotation movement. If you are using conventional stem binding which is self adhesive, squeeze the stem as you rotate it so that it sticks. Keep moving your hand down the stem until you have reached the bottom. There should be no need to move the hand holding the tape at all, because this would only slow down the process. When you reach the bottom of the stem simply twist the binding and break it off.

All the flower instructions are given in one fabric for simplicity, although a few alternative fabrics are suggested with some flowers. Really the choice, through experiment, depends entirely on the success of the fabric itself. As a rough guide, if you intend to make the particular flower in the sizes given, try to use the same weight of fabric. If you wish to vary the size of the flower, then of course you can vary the weight of the fabric accordingly.

In all flower making, attempt to conceal the manufacturing parts as much as possible and during petal assembly try to avoid touching the main part of the petal itself by handling it at the base only.

Be cautious with patterned fabrics as, apart from their inability in many cases to follow the growth marks on petals, they can be so bold as to conflict with and dominate the flower design.

1 Materials

An assortment of materials are assembled in this arrangement. Their various qualities from the rough hessian diagonal poppies to the fine organdie spiral bulrushes create a good contrast. There is a contrast in shape also with the real bulrushes which stand sentinal with ribbon and wired cotton poppies clustered in the centre.

With the wealth of materials available it would be virtually impossible to mention every type by name, so in describing the ones I am using I hope that this will give you incentive to experiment further with any other materials you think may be suitable. From silks and satins to hessians and felt, the weight and thickness of the materials can vary enormously. This thickness has to be incorporated in the design of the flowers and most particularly at the base of the petals where several layers tend to build up. As a general rule, therefore, if you intend to use a thick material, make a flower with only a few petals like a poppy and reserve lighter materials for flowers like roses and carnations. Having said this, there are so many flowers and fabrics that you should in no way feel restricted.

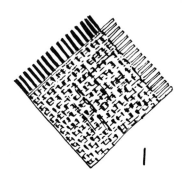

The very fact that a lot of fabrics are woven materials means that fraying can occur when shapes are cut; this is generally caused by the tension being released in the weave. Hessian, for example, where the fibre is coarse, springs out more easily than the more flimsy threads in organdie. Fraying is a hazard which has to be either controlled or incorporated into a flower design. In some tweed and hessians where two colours are woven across each other, an interesting effect can be achieved by fraying the edges purposely. At a chosen point you can secure the edges with glue, which will reveal each colour intensely where it frays (Fig 1). A thin coat of glue applied instantly to cut edges will prevent the start of fraying, as well as giving added strength to soft materials as it tends to harden as it dries. For example, the cotton poppies with their soft floppy petals would collapse completely without glue.

A hem, the conventional way of dealing with the edge of most materials, can also be a decorative feature of the design. The normal concealed stitches are perfectly acceptable in many cases but there are several embroidery stitches which could well be used instead (see Chapter 3). Edging stitches in contrasting thread simply incorporate the hem and wire frame as well, if there is one. Some fabrics have some kind of stiffening substance in their texture which prevents them from fraying easily, particularly if they are cut on the cross as is the case with tarlatan and organdie. It seems a shame to have to add a cumbersome hem to fine fabrics like silk and there is a form of iron-on interlining impregnated with glue made for hems. This can be used where the petals require no moulding, though of course you can incorporate a wire strengthener which would in turn support the petal in a gentle curve. Knitted fabrics are, on the whole, unsatisfactory for petals.

Choosing the colours for your flowers can be a time consuming process. If you are lucky enough to have a rag bag or remnants box through which to rummage, you will doubtless arrive at endless possibilities and colour combinations. It is surprising, in spite of the enormous range of colours, that if you are trying to match fabrics with natural plant material it can be a difficult task, so you may have to dye your own. A large range of both hot and cold water fabric dyes as well as bleaches is available. For a subtle match to your colour scheme it is, of course, possible to mix dyes of the same type together. You can make interesting experiments by varying the combinations slightly with each piece of fabric and you can also control the intensity of the dye either by the length of time you leave your fabric to soak or the strength of dye you mix up. So if you buy one piece of fabric you can, by your own adjustments of the dyes, achieve enough variation to fill a whole vase of flowers. Generally all the dyeing should be done and the fabric dried before the flowers are made up, so do make sure that you have in fact dyed enough material. You may find it extremely difficult to match up an exact colour a second time.

The edges of the petals can, however, be dyed after the flower is complete. Organdie roses can be particularly effective dyed in this way. For example white roses dipped into green dye (Fig 2) give the petals delicate green shadows, and daisies too are effective with coloured tips to their petals.

The batik method of dyeing is one which can be easily adapted to flower making. You can make a wealth of different patterns of your own choice rather than the somewhat regimented yardage patterns. There are many books and instruction leaflets available in the shops which give the techniques for batik dyeing, so simply follow the instructions and adapt the designs to suit your flower making.

Unlike most conventional uses of material where a symmetrical design has little or no part to play in the whole shape

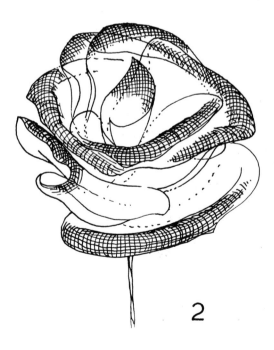

2

3

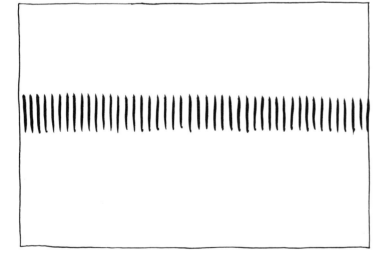

4

of the finished article, when you are making flowers it is the marks on the individual petals which, when assembled, complete the design of the flower. Therefore any mark you wish to make is a single component of a multiple design which generally radiates from the stem on which the flower grows. You should try not to make your design too complicated, because not only will a lot of unnecessary time be wasted but owing to the majority of petals overlapping in places, some of the marks will not even be seen.

The most simple pattern to make is achieved with random brush strokes with wax made with a coarse brush all over your material (Fig 3); then cut your petal shapes from it to make batik roses.

As a general rule, the marks you make should follow the direction of the petal lengthways. Where a flower appears to have stripes running across the petals, generally on close inspection the line will be made up of many small brush strokes beside each other (Fig 4). Patterns of this kind are found in pinks.

The patterns you can experiment with can be endless, from tipped and edged petals, splashes and dots to elaborate wriggly designs which can cover the entire petal. Batik is a fascinating technique but if you do not have the facilities for this method you can achieve alternative patterns by painting the dye on to your material with a brush.

For an instant effect, though they are not generally waterproof, felt tip pens are very easy tools to use. You will not be able to achieve the density of colour with the pens but you will have more control over finer marks. Only the lighter weight material in paler colours will allow the pen marks to be visible so experiment with your materials before you embark on a scheme. Dots of various sizes are the first marks which come to mind (Fig 5) and petals with this pattern occur in the lily family, especially the tiger lily.

Apart from the heavy textured materials, many others will require extra strength to maintain the petal position. There are several ways of doing this, firstly by mixing a solution of 1 tea-

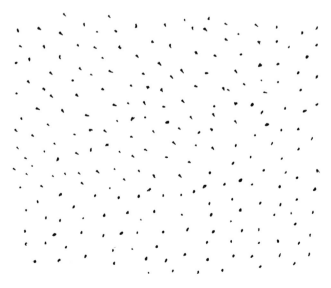

5

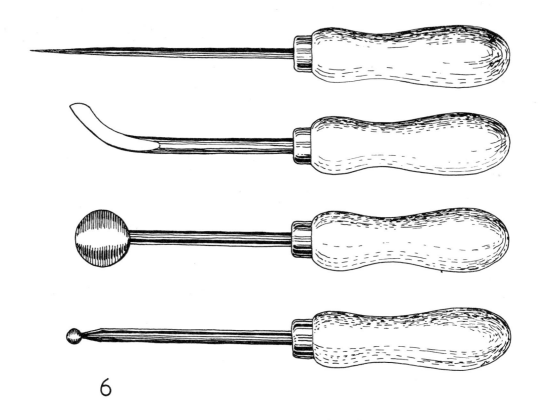

6

spoon gelatine to $\frac{1}{4}$ pint water, and then soaking the fabric until the solution has been thoroughly absorbed. Hang it out to dry and iron it before using it in the normal way, but remember that you should allow for shrinkage in the size of material you choose. This solution makes the fabrics quite crisp. You will find that the heat of the iron tends to soften it a little but it will stiffen again when it cools. It will now have a built-in adhesive to prevent fraying. This method of strengthening is used before you start making any flowers but there are two aerosols, one spray starch and the other spray varnish, both of which can be applied to a finished bloom. An attractive alternative, particularly if you intend to use candles with your flowers, is to dip your flowers into melted candle wax. Organdie flowers are particularly suitable and I would suggest that you only use white candle wax for perfect results. Once you have melted the wax, dip the flower head in and out very swiftly, then keep twisting it to prevent any blobs of wax forming on the petals as it cools. A few of these delicate translucent flowers with some red velvet ribbon and holly combine with candles for a dinner-table setting.

The fabric is not always used flat and by sewing it can be gathered, frilled or simply joined. It can, in the case of the lightweight materials, also be moulded like paper, over a knife or scissor blade. This process creates curls which can be applied to the edge of petals, but a shape in the centre can be made with a closed or open dart. Alternatively all kinds of cups, curls,

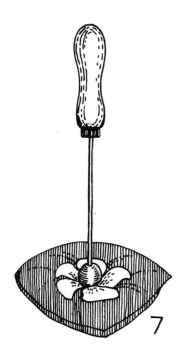

troughs and frills can be pressed into fabric with some flower irons (for suppliers see p 119). Although these add greatly to the realistic appearance of some flowers, they are by no means essential. In fact a few slight shapes can even be created with a conventional iron. However, if you intend to invest in some irons there is a whole set of various shapes and sizes (Fig 6) available, of which you could choose No 62 knife gouffer for troughs in daisy-type petals, No 82 ball gouffer for cup shapes, No 42 ball gouffer for small dents or No 46 carnation gouffer for rolled edges. The other irons would give you further variety within those shapes. To use the irons you will need a small hard cushion filled with horsehair or some similar material and a burner. I use a small camping gas burner which will stand on my work table. Also you should have a heatproof dish on which to lie your hot irons. First cut all the shapes you require, then hold an iron in the heat of the flame. Place one petal shape on the cushion and when you consider the iron to be hot enough press hard into the shape (Fig 7). You will find that the irons only retain their heat for a short while so simply re-heat them and continue shaping until you have completed the shape you require.

7

2 Centres

This basket holds three loop teazle tulips with plant material centres combined with wired disc flowers with raffia tassel centres. In the centre a cluster of hessian trumpets have bead centres, like the velvet arum lilies; the petersham dahlia has a frilly nylon ribbon centre.

The centre is the seed in the middle of the flower and essentially the whole reason for a flower being the shape it is. You can imitate or copy the centres or seeds from real flowers by using dried seedheads. From grasses and ferns to seedpods and fir cones, you can choose almost anything to complement the material you wish to use. Most dried plant material will require a wire stem. This is a simple process if there is a stem already as it can simply be bound to a stem wire (Fig 1) but if, like a fir cone for instance, you have to create one, make a hook on the top of a stem wire and weave it between the scales until it is secure, then straighten the stem (Fig 2). Seeds and pips, if they are soft enough to pierce with a pin, can then be pushed onto the top of stem wires with glue (Fig 3) or cradled in thin binding wire as you would tie a parcel, leaving two long ends to twist together for the stem (Fig 4), or finally in the case of tiny seeds, coat a styrofoam ball or puff ball in glue and press it into the seeds until they cover the surface (Fig 5). As a general guide try to make a contrast in texture by putting a fluffy grass with smooth material (Fig 6) and wooden seedpods, like fir cones, with fluffy material (Fig 7). By making these combinations the texture of both materials will be displayed to best advantage.

Another natural material which lends itself to flower making is feathers. Marabou feathers from turkeys are beautifully fluffy and just one or two could completely fill the centre of a flower with a profusion of fluff (Fig 8). For an exotic centre make a bunch of ostrich barbs from those luxurious plumes and allow

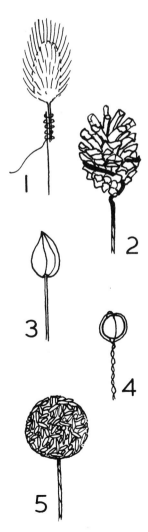

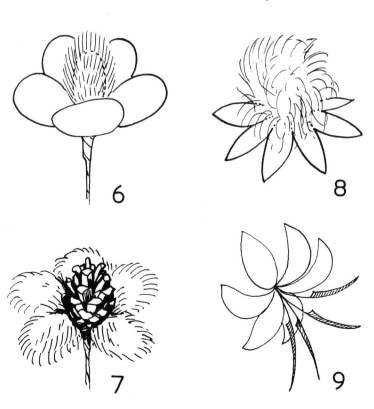

your flowers to have constantly drifting centres. For a more definite outline stiff wing feathers are ideal, particularly for the pendant type of flower. They will spring out into a fan if they are bound very tightly to a stem (Fig 9). Some feathers are too solid to use in this way, so simply strip off the unwanted lower part of the feather before you use it.

Where the centre is to hang below the flower itself, the outline will be completely visible. For this you can use tassels, either those found on lampshade fringing (Fig 10) or make your own. Any thread will do as long as it is soft and manageable. Use five pencils, or adjust the number according to the size of tassel you require, and wind the thread round until you have sufficient thickness (Fig 11). Thread a piece of wire through the binding and tie it tightly before you slip out the pencils (Fig 12). Then bind the loops together near to the point where they are wired (Fig 13), finish off with a neat knot and cut all the loops (Fig 14).

If you require a more simple pendant centre you can just make knots at the end of some cords and make a bunch of several of varying lengths (Fig 15). This is a good method when you require a lot of stamens. Conversely for a dramatic effect with heavy material petals, you could use thick cord and make one stamen with a big knot on the end (Fig 16).

Beads in their immense variety are excellent objects for seeds and stamens of all kinds. Whether they are made of wood, pearl, ivory, or glass, their firm outline makes a good contrast to fabric petals. Whether they are clustered into the centre of a sunflower (Fig 17) or standing on the end of wire stems in a water lily (Fig 18), their positive outline is instantly recognisable. For the tiniest flowers one single bead makes an ideal centre (Fig 19) and if it is a glass one there will be the addition of a tiny sparkle in the centre of each flower.

Sequins, with almost as many uses as beads, would also sparkle in the centre. This is a point to remember if you are proposing to use your flowers in artificial or candlelight. Very economical to use, sequins in large numbers will cluster happily in the centre of a flower or can be suspended for a pendant type. There are, however, some glass drop beads which particularly lend themselves to this type of flower (Fig 20). Sequin shapes of various designs can also be used or indeed combined with beads to make interesting features.

To contrast with the multiple centres with many beads or sequins, often one bead, large or small, will create the desired effect. You can use a bobble from a lampshade fringe or make the raffia berry, both adding texture to a simple shape in the centre. If however you would prefer not to deviate from the materials you are using for the petals, you can cover a puff ball with it like the grapes. By this method you can choose many other materials too; a stretchy fabric like jersey knit makes a

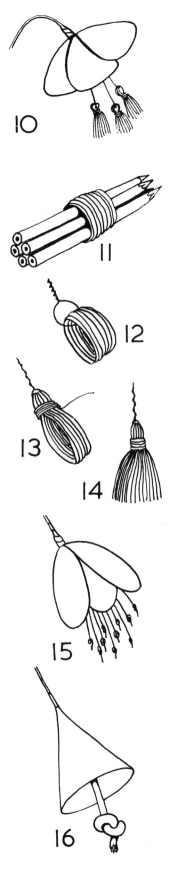

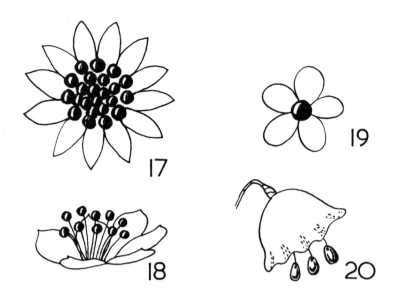

very neat covering or, a little more cumbersome but very effective, is fur fabric.

Whatever type of centre you decide to make, consider at the same time the design of your whole flower. Contrast of texture and tone are important components. The size of your centre relates directly to that of your petal, which, if laid flat, should just be visible all round. The numbers of one to the other should also be relative; for example, where there is more than one stamen, the number of petals should be a multiple of the centre. So if you have six stamens you should make six or twelve petals rather than ten, though of course if you have one seed in the centre the number of petals can be endless.

3 Embroidery for Decoration

This little trough supports the flowers and is made of plate mirror glass, which is a reflective container for the embroidered hollyhocks and couched leaves. The arrangement is then filled with an assortment of dried plant material, teazels, and artichoke and wild oats.

1

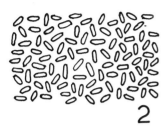

2

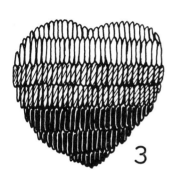

3

Many materials are entirely patterned and consequently the uniformity of design adds little more than overall colouring to a flower. Therefore do not consider your embroidery in the light of pattern making but more to emphasise flower growth, or as a texture to add to the surface. Handmade things have the charm of being slightly irregular at times, a quality which only adds to the natural appearance of a flower, so do not let this deter you from adding this individual touch. Whether in the centre of leaves and petals, or round the edge, there are numerous stitches which are worth trying. Your embroidery should be a series of marks which go to make up the whole, rather than obvious floral stitches which tend to be too complete in themselves.

The simplest embroidery design of all is to work with a constant thread and make one little line with each stitch you make. Then just how many and where you place them determines the pattern you create. Join your little stitches in a line and you have back stitch, put them side by side and you have satin stitch (Fig 1). Slightly overlap them and you have stem stitch, or put them higgledy piggledy all over and you have seed stitch (Fig 2). Of all these, satin stitch can be very rich in the centre of a flower, particularly if the colours are shaded deeper in the middle (Fig 3). An interesting variation on this is feather stitch which has alternately long and short stitches which allow the integration of adjoining colours; you can make a series of 'V' shapes either touching or set apart like veining (Fig 4). Another useful stitch for patterning fabric is the French knot (Fig 5).

One of the oldest stitches is the cross stitch or sampler stitch, the basic shape being easily recognisable. It can either be made individually or as several in a row to create a solid line (Fig 6).

4

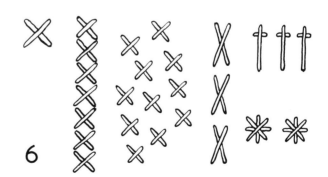

6

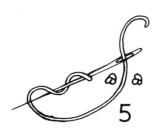

5

Indeed as a pattern it is possible to make cross stitch filling by spacing them evenly over the given area. You could vary the angle of the crosses or make differing lengths to the arms in a stitch, called long armed cross stitch. The double cross stitch speaks for itself and an interesting variation would be to make this one in two colours. If you have a large area to fill you could make one of the cross stitches used in rug making, that is a single cross stitch with an extra stitch across each arm (Fig 7). Some of our old embroidery stitches had lovely names. I like particularly ermine stitch; this is again another form of cross stitch but as the name suggests they would make elegant patterns in black on a white background (Fig 8).

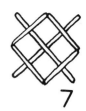

Daisy stitch, by its very name, suggests that it should be used for flower decoration. The shape of the basic stitch (Fig 9) echoes the shape of a lot of petals. Whether you choose to put one or several depends on the design of your flower, but they need not necessarily be the same size, and the catch stitch can be of variable length (Fig 10).

All the designs and stitches so far have simply produced a mark in the centre part of the leaf or petal. There are a great many alternatives to be found in the many stitches in lines or edging stitches. To continue by the same method as the daisy stitch, you simply link one inside the other to make chain stitch closed, or separate the ends and it is open (Fig 11). Blanket stitch is the other one which springs to mind, not only as decoration but serving a useful purpose of sewing fabric to a wire frame. There are many variations to choose from, all of which make excellent edging stitches (Fig 12). Overstitch may seem an ob-

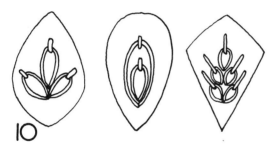

viously simple edge to do but it is effective and efficient also for wire frames (Fig 13). You could also use this stitch for couching either another decorative thread to the surface, or indeed a wire stem (Fig 14).

Having suggested several of the simplest embroidery stitches to try, there are a few more elaborate and beautifully decorative stitches for the experienced needlewoman who I am sure will interpret the suggestions in the diagram (Fig 15).

As the embroidery is a decorative addition to the flowers you will not find any stitches suggested in the flower instructions themselves, so that part of design consideration is left to your choice.

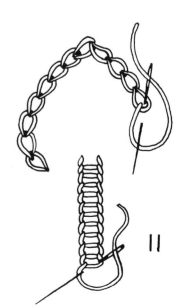

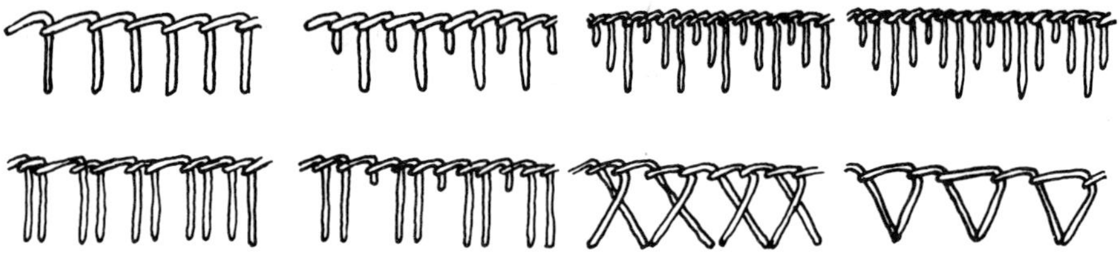

12

13

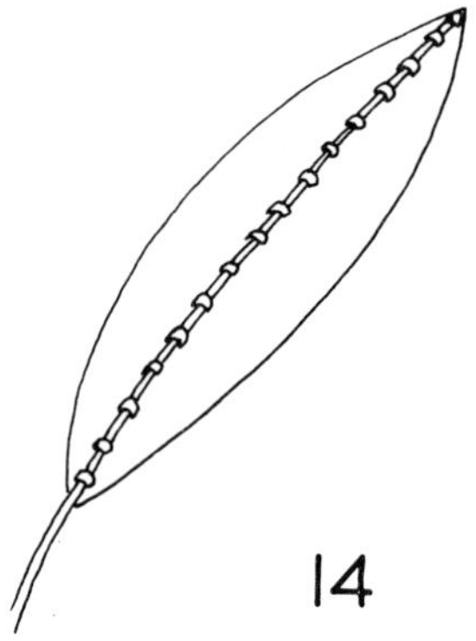

14

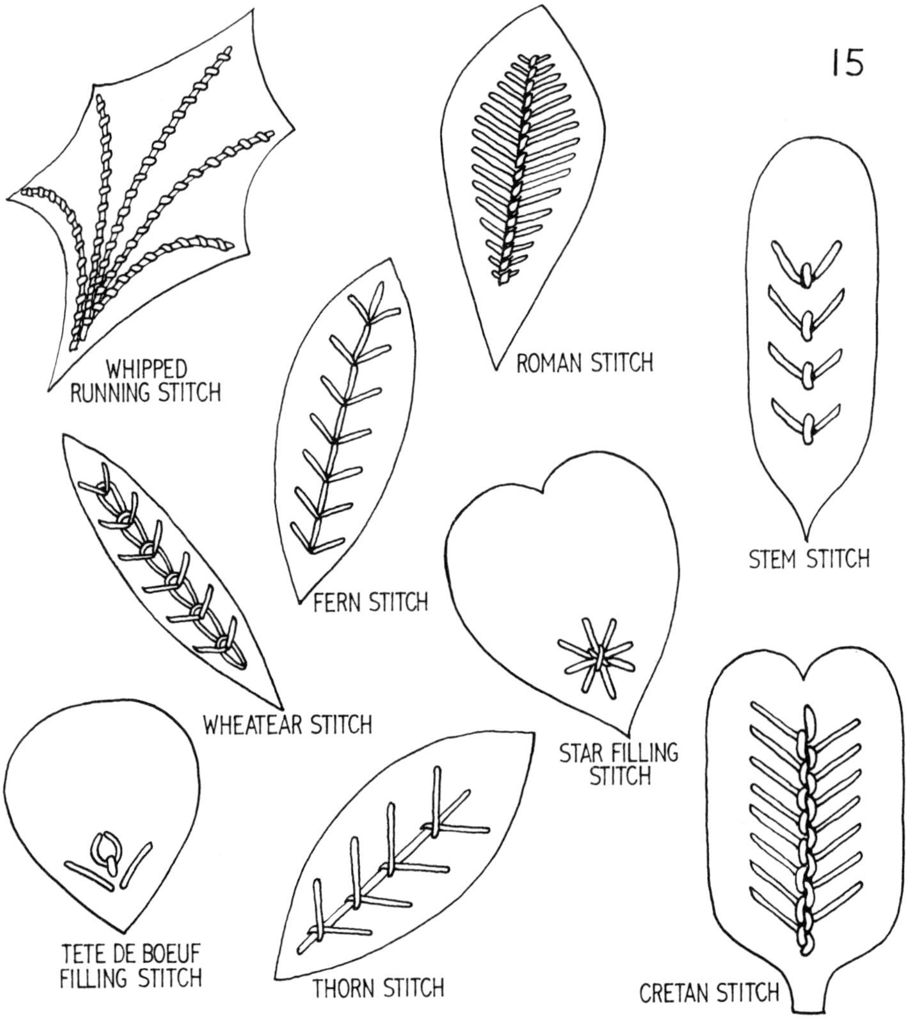

15

WHIPPED
RUNNING STITCH

ROMAN STITCH

STEM STITCH

FERN STITCH

WHEATEAR STITCH

STAR FILLING
STITCH

TETE DE BOEUF
FILLING STITCH

THORN STITCH

CRETAN STITCH

4 Ribbon and Raffia Flowers

This is a spray of lace flowers arranged decoratively with velvet leaves which are made in the same way as the couched leaves but the wire runs between the layers of fabric.

Sun daisy

Fabric: Choose two shades of raffia. You will need 48cm (18in) of one shade and 72cm (27in) of the other. Carefully ease out the creases until the raffia is flat and as wide as possible.

Shapes: Cut six strips of 8cm (3in) from the shorter length and six strips of 12cm (4½in) from the long one. Twist the centre of one piece, like a toffee wrapping, keeping the ends as flat as possible (Fig 1). Then double the shape over and twist the open ends together, holding the centre part as flat as possible (Fig 2). Repeat this with all the remaining strips – you will find that if you twist them firmly enough they will stay in place while you are shaping the others.

Centre: Use a bunch of 6 bought stamens (Fig 3). As these have a globule on each end, fold them in half to double the number and bind the folded ends to the top of a stem wire (Fig 4).

Petals: Use the smallest petals first and bind them individually to the centre, spacing them evenly all round. Then add the larger petals in exactly the same way.

Stem: Cover the base of the petals and the stem. As this is a daisy the flowerhead should stand flat on top of a vertical stem.

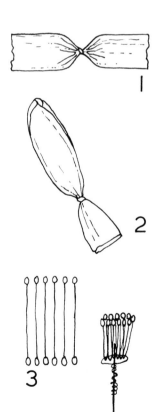

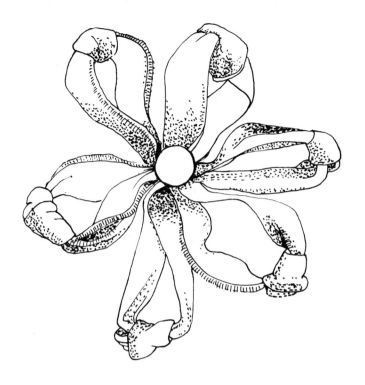

Knotted daisy

Fabric: A fairly stiff ribbon is required for the petals of this daisy because they must support their own shape without any additional material. Thin velvet ribbon is the most suitable as the surface pile gives a third dimension.

Shapes: Cut six pieces 18cm (7in) long and tie a knot in the centre of each one (Fig 1).

Centre: Use an artificial fruit, like a cherry for example, and bind the stem of it to a stem wire (Fig 2).

Petals: Join the ends of each of the knotted ribbon strips together with a piece of binding wire (Fig 3). Bind them to the centre separately, arranging them evenly as you do so.

Stem: Cover the base of the petals and the stem with binding tape.

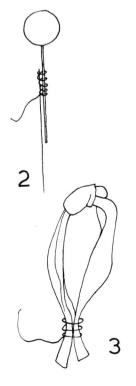

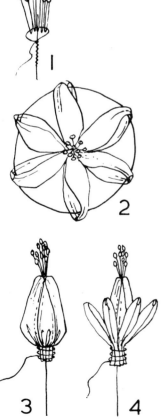

Fuchsia

Fabric: Raffia is used for the fuchsia so choose two tones, preferably in the pink to purple range.

Shapes: For instructions for the preparation of the petals, follow the sun daisy as the numbers and dimensions are exactly the same.

Centre: Use 5 bought stamens, double them over and bind them tightly to the top of a stem wire (Fig 1).

Petals: Use the smallest petals first and bind each one individually to the centre, taking care to space them evenly. Thread a small length of binding wire through the loop in each petal (Fig 2) and twist the ends of the wire together. This should draw the ends of the petals in to form a bud around the stamens (Fig 3). Add the remaining petals with binding wire, but arrange them as you do so, so that they encircle the bud evenly (Fig 4).

Stem: Cover the base of the petals and the stem. Bend the stem over 4cm (1½in) below the flower so that the head is pendulous.

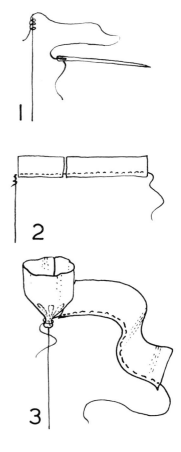

Jonquil

Fabric: You will need inch wide nylon ribbon in two colours, one 7cm (2½in) long and the other 13cm (5in).

Shapes: The ribbon is used just as it comes and requires no shaping.

Centre: Attach one end of binding wire to a stem wire and thread a needle onto the other (Fig 1).

Petals: Simply gather first the short length, then the long one on the same wire (Fig 2). Push them up tightly together so that they encircle the stem once for each ribbon and secure the end (Fig 3). Join the loose ends of ribbon with a little glue.

Stem: Cover the base of the petals and the stem, then kink the stem so that the little flower faces forwards.

Alternative fabrics: Any contrasting ribbon could be used other than petersham which would be too heavy. Unusual combinations could result with plain and patterned ribbons.

Colour Plate 1
In this arrangement in a little china urn from Italy, all the flowers and leaves are transparent. Organdie is used for the twisted flower in the centre, the organdie cups across the top and the four little harebells. The skeleton magnolia leaves are dyed green to complement the colour of the sequins used.

Colour Plate 2
In this antique container
the flowers are modern in
design. The contrast of
colour, texture and shape
can be clearly seen. The furry
bulrushes stand sentinel
between the pointed petals
of the petersham dahlias.
Deep turquoise shiny silk was
chosen for the disc leaves, to
show off the gathers on them.

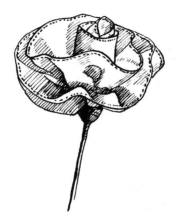

Little ribbon rose and bud

Fabric: You will need nylon ribbon an inch wide for both the little rose and the bud.

Shapes: Cut a 21cm (8in) length for the rose and a 11cm (4in) length for the bud.

Centre: Join one end of a piece of binding wire to a stem wire and a needle to the other, both for the rose and the bud (Fig 1).

Rose: Gather the longest piece of ribbon onto the wire (Fig 2) and bind it round the stem so that it forms a spiral before you secure the end.

Bud: Assemble in exactly the same way as the rose but allow the ribbon to encircle the stem only once.

Alternative fabric: Velvet ribbon makes a rich substitute for this flower.

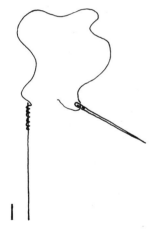

I

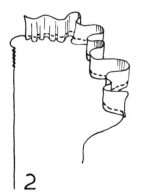

2

Petersham dahlia

Fabric: You will need 2 lengths of inch wide nylon ribbon 54cm (21in) long in different toning shades for the centre. Also a 45cm (18in) length of 2in wide petersham ribbon for the petals.

Shapes: Cut the petersham across in a V shape rather than straight (Fig 1) so that you have 6 equal sized pieces.

Centre: Join a piece of binding wire to the top of a stem wire (Fig 2) and gather both lengths of nylon ribbon together. Push them up tightly and bind onto the stem wire (Fig 3).

Petals: Continue with the same piece of binding wire to thread the point of each of the six petals (Fig 4). Secure the end of the wire to the stem. Join each adjoining lower edge together (Fig 5) – this will prevent the petals from overlapping.

Stem: Cover the stem with binding tape. You may find that the weight of this flower requires extra support. If so, add another stem wire to the first and bind the stem again.

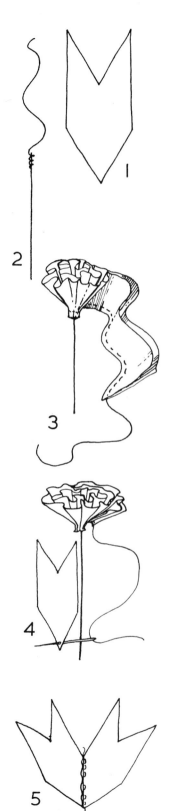

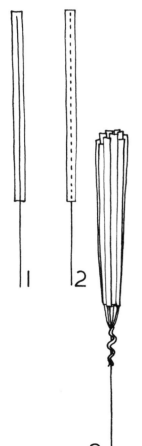

Chrysanthemum

Fabric: Velvet ribbon ⅜in wide is the best to choose for this flower. You will need two colours 205cm (80in) of each.

Shapes: Cut both ribbons into ten pieces 20·5cm (8in) long. Apply glue to the underside of one piece and place a 25cm (10in) piece of binding wire up the centre (Fig 1). Then put a piece of the other coloured ribbon onto it, sandwiching the wire in the centre (Fig 2). Repeat this until you have ten petals.

Centre: Join a piece of binding wire to the top of a stem wire.

Petals: Bind all the petals on at the same time to the stem wire (Fig 3) and secure the binding.

Stem: Cover the stem with binding tape. Bend each petal into a spiral shape until the whole flower head is a mass of curly petals.

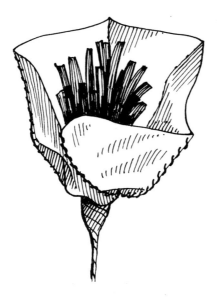

Lampshade flower

Fabric: You will need 30cm (10in) of inch wide corded ribbon, or fairly stiff ribbon. Do not use nylon as it is too flimsy, or velvet which is too cumbersome, but satin ribbon would be satisfactory. Raffia is used for the tassel in the centre.

Shapes: Cut five pieces, 6cm (2in) long and sew them all together side by side until you have a tube (Fig 1).

Centre: The raffia is used for a home-made tassel (Fig 2) as described in Chapter 2.

Petals: Place the ribbon tube over the centre and bind it tightly to the stem wire below the tassel, gathering the ribbon in as you do so.

Stem: Cover the base of the petals and the stem with binding tape. As it is comparatively simple to make these flowers in quantity, you could make several and join them together into a spray. Do this by simply binding one with binding tape and then adding another further down the stem. No further binding wire should be required as the binding tape is normally sufficient.

1

2

Simple raffia flower

Fabric: Choose one shade of raffia and in making your decision consider that the raffia is to be stretched out and so becomes translucent and paler. For the centre you will need eight toning small glass beads.

Shapes: Cut eight strips of 8cm (3¼in) from the raffia and twist the centre of each, then twist the ends together as for the sun daisy.

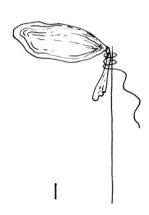

Petals: As the centre is added after the assembly of the petals, join a piece of binding wire to the top of a stem wire. Place each petal separately and bind it tightly to the stem (Fig 1) and continue to add the rest arranging them evenly around the stem. Then flatten the top of the flower and glue the little beads in a cluster in the centre.

Stem: Finally cover the base of the petals and the stem with binding tape, taking care to keep the stem straight.

Frilly flower

Fabric: This particular flower has been made with nylon ribbon, but satin, velvet or any other flexible ribbon would be equally successful.

Shape: Cut one piece 41cm (16in) long.

Petals: Thread a needle with a piece of binding wire and secure the loose end to the top of a stem wire. Gather along one long side of the ribbon and pull it up (Fig 1). Immediately the end nearest the centre will have formed a coil around the stem wire, so continue to bind the rest of the frilled ribbon into place, easing in the gathering as you do so to keep the outline of the flower as circular as possible.

Stem: Cover the base of the petals and stem with binding tape.

Variation: There is a lace edging which is already frilled and which would make a pretty substitute for the ribbon.

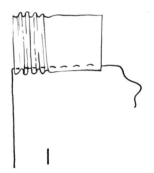

1

Lace flower

Fabric: A visit to the haberdashery department will provide the components for this little flower. The petals are made with lace trimmings 3cm (1in) wide and the centre is a tassel from a lampshade fringe.

Shape: Cut a strip 11cm ($4\frac{1}{2}$in) long from the lace.

Centre: Cut a tassel from the fringe, thread a piece of binding wire through the loop and bind it to the top of a stem wire (Fig 1).

Petals: Leave the end of the binding wire on for the petals. Thread a needle onto the end, sew along the edges of the lace (Fig 2) and pull it up. Bind it to the stem so that the lace forms a single cup.

Stem: Cover the base of the petals and stem with binding tape.

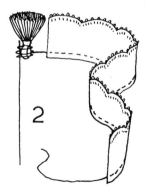

5 Silk, Satin and Velvet Flowers

All the flowers and leaves are made of silk. There are five convolvulus
combined with silk roses and wired disc leaves. The Victorian egret feathers
form a delicate tracery to set off the flowers.

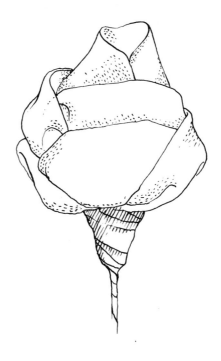

Silk rose

Fabric: As all the petals are folded double for this rose, try to find the finest silk that you can to avoid the flower becoming too cumbersome.

Shapes: Cut six diamond shapes 8cm (3in) long and 6cm (2½in) wide from your fabric (Fig 1) noting the direction of the weave.

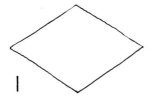

Centre: Join a piece of binding wire to a stem wire. Fold one of the pieces in half diagonally to make a triangle and fold the two side points over, one on top of the other (Fig 2). This will have formed a cone shape. Gather all the loose edges together by hand (Fig 3) and, holding it tightly bunched together, bind it to the stem wire.

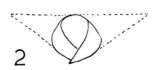

Petals: Fold each of the other pieces diagonally in half, similar to the centre. Fold one around the centre to encase it (Fig 4) and gather it in as you bind it to the stem (Fig 5). The petal should wrap around the centre and each following petal should overlap the previous one by half. This flower is not particularly easy to make but firm handling will help and will also ensure the binding to be as compact as possible.

Stem: Cover the base of petals and the stem with binding tape.

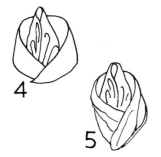

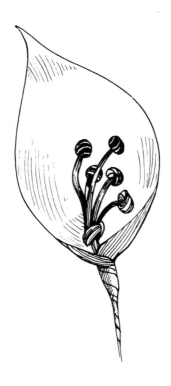

Silk arum lily

Fabric: As silk tends to fray the petal of this lily is made of two layers joined together with bondina. The shape of this coiled petal can cradle the most fragile of centres. In this case they are a bunch of little raffia berries on their own raffia stems.

Shapes: Take the two pieces of silk and one of bondina; sandwich the bondina in the centre and iron the three layers together. From this thick piece cut one pointed petal shape, 10cm (4in) by 7cm (2½in) (Fig 1).

Centre: Make five raffia berries as described in Chapter 8 and tie their raffia stems together in a knot (Fig 2), arranging them so that they are of different lengths. Bind the bunch to a stem wire so that the knot is just above the top of it.

Petals: Coil the petal shape round so that the base just overlaps and place it around the stem so that the centre lies in the middle of the petal. Secure firmly with binding wire.

Stem: Cover the base of the petal and the stem with binding tape.

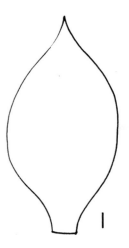

1

2

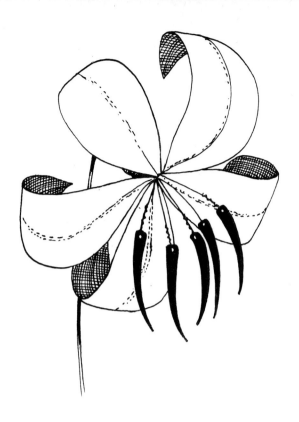

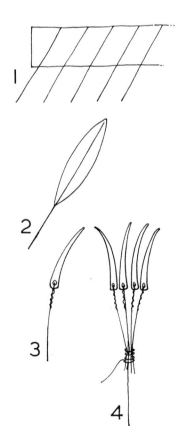

Two-tone tiger lily

Fabric: The two colours you can see in this flower are really two separate pieces of material, preferably silk, joined together with bondina, and this shape of flower lends itself to exotic pendulous stamens. In this case they are shaped sequins.

Shapes: Cut five lengths of binding wire 15cm (6in) long and place them diagonally in a row on one piece of the coloured silk (Fig 1). Then put the bondina on top and finally the other piece of silk, and press the whole flat with a warm iron. Now cut out five pointed oval shapes, measuring 11cm (4in) by 3cm (1in), making sure that the wire goes up the centre of each shape (Fig 2).

Centre: Thread each one of the five shaped sequins on a piece of binding wire and twist the end back on itself (Fig 3). Join them together in a bunch of even lengths and bind them to the top of the stem wire (Fig 4).

Petals: Arrange the petals around the centre evenly and bind tightly with binding wire.

Stem: Cover the base of the petals and the stem with binding tape. Curl each of the petals outwards around your finger to form a tiger lily shape, and finally bend the head of the flower over so that the stamens hang down.

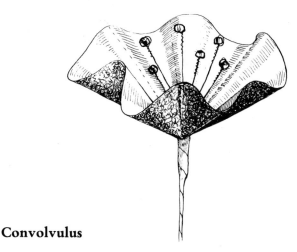

Convolvulus

Fabric: You will need silk and some iron-on vilene for the convolvulus. The weight of material you choose will depend on the thickness of the covered stem wire which serves to hold the petals in place.

Shapes: Cut two discs, one in silk and the other from vilene 20cm (8in) in diameter, and make a small hole in the centre of the vilene.

Centre: You will need six beads for the stamens. Thread each one onto a piece of binding wire separately and secure on the top by twisting the ends of the wire back on itself. Make a bunch keeping them all the same length, about 10cm (4in), and bind them to the top of a stem wire. Fan them out equally (Fig 1).

Petals: Cut six pieces of covered stem wire 13cm (5in) long, bind them together on their own allowing 10cm (4in) free at the top. Fan them out until they radiate on a flat surface (Fig 2). Next place the piece of silk onto the ironing board, then the wires (Fig 3) followed by the vilene. Press the bound ends of the wire through the hole in the centre (Fig 4). Press the assembled layers together keeping the wires equally spaced as you do so. Cut between one of the wires right into the centre and ease the wires together to allow the fabric to drape down in between.

Stem: Cover the base of the petals and the stem with binding tape. This flower has so many wires within its structure that you may well have to add extra stem wires to the original to support the flower head. Do this by placing them alongside and covering them altogether with binding tape.

Variations: It is possible to make this flower with any light fabric that will withstand the heat of the iron. Try ironing a sample before cutting out any petals. Plain or patterned cottons are suitable but do not choose a pattern that dominates the appearance of the flower to the extent that it distorts the shape. eg Stripes.

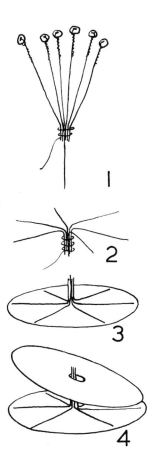

Velvet Camellia

Fabric: As the title suggests you will need some velvet. There is some moulding in this flower so first dip the velvet you intend to use in gelatine solution. Iron it on the reverse side when almost dry.

Shapes: Cut three discs from the fabric, one 8cm (3in) wide, another 6·5cm (2½in) and the third 5cm (2in) wide, and at four equidistant points around the edge, cut out pointed notches (Fig 1). Using the flower-making iron No 82, press a hollow in the centre of each piece on the right side (Fig 2). Then using iron No 42 turn the petals over and press a trough along the edge (Fig 3).

Centre: Use ready-made stamens in the centre. These are the type with a blob on both ends, so fold a small bunch of them in half and bind to the top of a stem wire (Fig 4).

Petals: Thread the smallest one onto the stem wire, using the wire to force a hole big enough to thread the petal on. Bind this to the stem gathering the disc together as you do so (Fig 5). Attach the medium-sized petal next in exactly the same way and follow with the largest afterwards.

Stem: Cover the base of the petals and the stem with binding tape. As the tapering shape of the base of the petals is difficult to cover, ensure that you have done so before you cover the stem.

Variations: Although it is very unusual to see a real camellia with petals in various shades, it can look effective if the centre petal is a different shade, or colour. You may also require a giant flower and this is one of the flower designs which is very easily adaptable. The size at which you finally arrive will only otherwise be governed by the strength of the material you choose. Those who are practised in the art of flower making will recognise this simple petal shape in large tissue-paper flowers, but these will be far superior owing to the texture displayed in the moulded velvet.

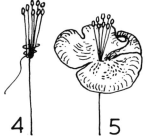

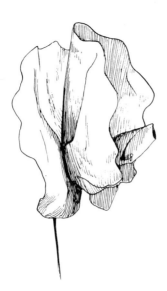

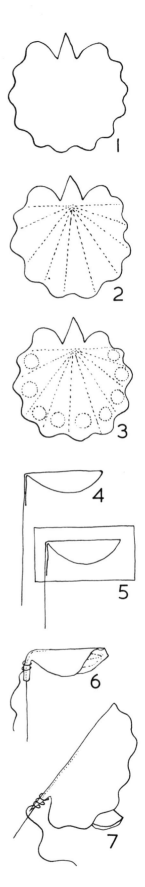

Sweet pea

Fabric: Taffeta – in fact this one has been made from lining material rather than using the most expensive material, and is found to be perfectly satisfactory. This flower requires moulding so dip the material in a gelatine solution and iron it flat when almost dry.

Shapes: Cut three discs 10cm (4in) in diameter and then shape the edges by cutting round them a second time to make a wavy edge. Then at one point on the edge cut out the shape of a W (Fig 1). Using flower-making iron No 62 press radiating troughs to about ten points around the edge (Fig 2). Then with iron No 42 turn the petals over and press hollows between the ends of each line (Fig 3).

Centre: Cut an oblong piece of the same fabric 8cm (3in) by 5cm (2in). Use a piece of covered stem wire to make a framework on which to construct the centre. Cut a piece of wire 13cm (5in) long and fold it in half to make a loop and bind the ends to the top of a stem wire. Bend the loop forwards and flatten the top of it (Fig 4). Place the wire shape onto the piece of fabric so that the tip lies just in from the centre of one of the 5cm (2in) sides (Fig 5). Fold the fabric over at this point, then continue wrapping the loop with the remaining fabric (Fig 6).

Petals: Place one of the petals behind the centre and fold it in half so that it encases the centre between the fold. The little point in the centre should lie directly behind the centre of the stem. Bind this little piece to the stem taking care not to trap any of the rest of the petals in with it (Fig 7). Add the second petal behind the first in exactly the same way, but do not fold it.

Stem: Cover the base of the petals and the stem with binding tape. To make the flower face forward bend the stem just below the base of the petals until it is at a right angle.

Variations: As the particular fabric has been chosen this does not rule out the possibilities of using several other types with equal success. Organdie, in particular, is ideal. With this and other slightly transparent fabrics an interesting effect can be achieved by making the front and first petal in a different shade.

Thomas's flower

Fabric: Taffeta is the best material but even lining material is satisfactory which makes this a very economical flower to make. When you have chosen the material you wish to use, soak it in a gelatine solution and iron it flat when almost dry. There is no moulding in this flower but the gelatine not only gives a little body strength to the material but translucency as well. This particular flower is made with white taffeta with the hint of colour created by using a coloured table jelly for the solution.

Shapes: Cut two discs 12cm (4½in) in diameter, then trim round the edge again to give the shape a wavy outline (Fig 1). Cut a third disc 5cm (2in) in diameter.

Centre: First cover a stem wire with binding tape, then apply glue to the top before sticking a puff ball to it. When it is dry, use the small disc to cover the ball and bind the free edges as close to the ball as possible so that it neatly covers it (Fig 2).

Petals: Fold each of the discs in half and place one inside the other but allow the inside one to protrude to one side (Fig 3). Place a piece of binding wire in the fold and bind it to the centre allowing the piece to form a coil around it (Fig 4).

Stem: Cover the base of the petals and, for the second time, the stem. If you make your binding as tight as possible the second binding should not prove to be too unsightly. Ease the petals apart so that the layers are clearly visible.

Variations: This is a flower which can be one of the giant variety, and will be governed by not only the strength of the fabric but the number of petals you use. You will find the larger the flower you require, the larger the number of petals will be required to keep the shape. Several colours can be used to advantage in the flower, particularly if you put a large number of petals. Organdie is an excellent alternative to use allowing, through the translucency of the fabric, the various colours to merge together. Sprays of tiny bells can be quickly made using this flower pattern. Use only one disc for each little coil, which can be successfully as small as 6cm (2½in) in diameter. Make each one on a separate short stem, assemble into a spray, then curve each little stem over so that not only the bell shapes hang down but the whole stem curves slightly.

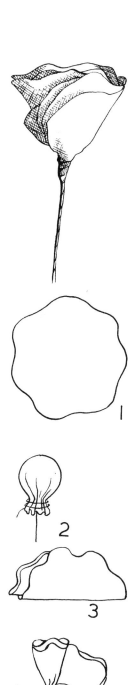

49

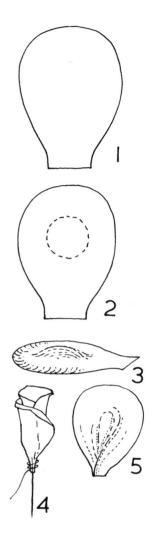

Two-tone rose

Fabric: The peculiar quality in this rose is achieved by the use of two-tone millium, lining material. Although moulding is required for the shapes of the petals, the material is quite stiff enough to hold the shape without the gelatine solution.

Shapes: You will need twelve petals for this rose. They are divided into three groups, one of two, one of three and the other of seven petals. Cut the first group in an arch shape 5cm (2in) high narrowing to 2cm ($\frac{3}{4}$in) at the base. The second group should be the same shape but 5·5cm (2$\frac{1}{4}$in) high and 2cm ($\frac{3}{4}$in) at the base. The final group is the same again but 6·5cm (2$\frac{1}{2}$in) high and 2cm ($\frac{3}{4}$in) at the base (Fig 1). Mould the first group, pale side up, with flower iron No 82 in the centre and press a hollow (Fig 2) turn the fabric over and, with iron No 42, make a trough all round the arch (Fig 3) and to emphasise the shape use flower iron No 46 and run it along the trough.

Centre: Use the petals from the first group, take one, roll it up like a cigarette and bind it tightly to the top of a stem wire. Then add a further one by wrapping it round the first, and the third in a similar fashion (Fig 4).

Petals: Use the petals from the third group next and add each one separately, overlapping the previous one by half each time. As you assemble the flower the outside petals will require a small pleat at the base to prevent them from falling open (Fig 5).

Stem: Cover the base of the petals and the stem with binding tape. A rose has a fairly rigid stem so there should be no need to bend it.

Colour Plate 3
The colours of this arrangement in a gold candlestick are natural shades of green and gold. The hessian weave used for the five diagonal poppies is a combination of these two, and the colour scheme is continued in the golden barley and green butcher's broom.

Colour Plate 4
This formal arrangement
of peacock tail feathers,
two-tone roses, and chiffon
arum lilies, is displayed in a
green marble vase supported
by three dolphins. The
chocolate and ivory fabrics
used for those flowers
are combined with
turquoise velvet rose buds and
grapes which pick out the
iridescent colour of the
peacock feathers.

Batik carnation

Fabric: The batik method gives the reason for using silk for the carnation. It is one of the many-petalled flowers, so do not choose a silk which is too thick and bulky. At the same time, however, there is no moulding or any other form of support so the silk must be substantial enough to support itself. Apply the batik design by making a line of splashes (as described in Chapter 1).

Shapes: Cut a strip of material 69cm (27in) by 6cm (2in) so that the batik design gives a contrasting colour across the top (Fig 1). Gather along the length of the fabric with binding wire.

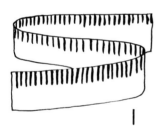

Centre: Attach a dried love-in-a-mist seed to the stem wire (Fig 2).

Petals: Bind the gathered petals around the seed centre as tightly as possible with the other end of the binding wire.

Stem: Cover the base of the petals and the stem with binding tape. Separate the layers of frilly petals.

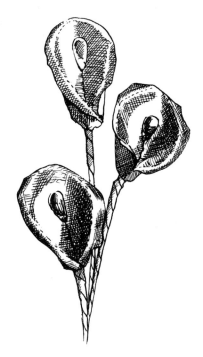

Two-tone lily spray

Fabric: The essential quality of these lilies is achieved by the use of two-toned fabric, one that has a contrast on the reverse. Two-toned millium lining material is the type to use, as used for the two-tone roses.

Shapes: Cut three pieces approx 4cm (1½in) by 6cm (2¼in) with rounded tops (Fig 1). Mould each one with flower iron No 82 and make a hollow in the centre of each one, then turn them over and make a trough along each side with iron No 42.

Centre: Use a bead for the centre and thread one onto a piece of binding wire, secure the end by twisting the end of the wire back on itself and then join it to the top of a stem wire (Fig 2). Repeat this for the two other flowers.

Petals: Make a pleat at the base of one of the petals and bind it round the centre so that the bead is clearly visible in the centre (Fig 3). Ensure that you only let the petal overlap slightly at the base, and to do this you may have to gather the back of the petal as well as the pleat; it will depend on the width of the base of your petal. Repeat the process with the other two petals on the other two centres.

Stem: Cover the base of the petals and the stem with binding tape. Then assemble the spray by placing one beside another so that that one is lower than the other at a point where the top of one touches the bottom of the one above. Bind the two stems together with binding tape. Repeat the process with the last one and cover the stem again.

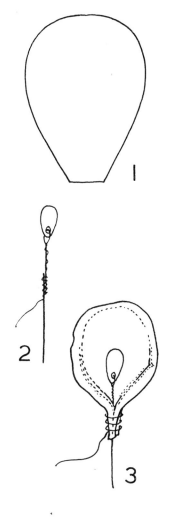

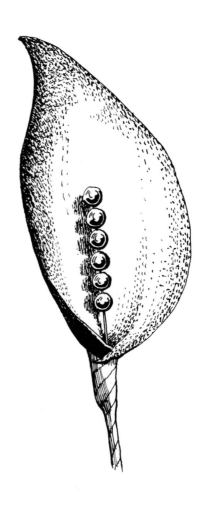

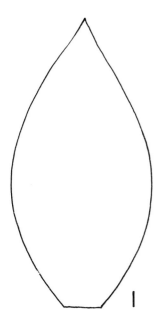

Velvet arum lily

Fabric: The texture of the velvet is shown to best advantage in this flower, almost more than any other. The curve of the single petal which catches the light from various angles contributes to the final affect, though to hold the shape it should first be dipped into a gelatine solution.

Shapes: Cut one pointed oval shape 18cm (7in) long and 9cm (3½in) wide (Fig 1). Shape the centre with flower iron No 82 to make a cup shape, then with iron No 42 to roll the sides of the two top edges outwards.

Centre: Thread six gold beads onto a covered stem wire and secure the top and bottom with a little glue.

Petals: Curve the petal around the stem so that the beads lie in the centre of the petal and the petal only just overlaps, then secure with binding wire.

Stem: If the weight of the flower head bends the stem, add one or two more stem wires beside the original. Then cover the base of the petal and the stem wires with binding tape.

6 Organandie, Net and Chiffon Flowers

The severe outline of the black shaped sequins in the centre of the two-toned tiger lilies, is echoed by the silk arum lilies. This allows the texture of the pom-pom flowers to be shown to best advantage in the dolphin candlestick container.

Stem of buds

Fabric: There are several flowers which are variations of the method used here in the spray of buds. These are organdie but it is interesting to see how the appearance varies with the different fabrics.

Shapes: Cut a diamond shaped piece 14cm (5½in) long and 11cm (4in) wide (Fig 1). Fold in half diagonally.

Centre: As there are five identical buds on this stem, the instructions are given for one and the others will simply be a repetition of the first. Choose a glixia as the centre and attach it to a short stem wire with binding wire, allowing 4cm (1½in) of stem (Fig 2).

Petals: Join the left hand point of the fold first to the stem wire and ease the fabric into the binding so that the end only just overlaps the beginning. The little glixia should be clearly visible in the centre (Fig 3).

Stem: When you have all the little buds complete, join the first one to the top of a stem wire with binding wire. Bind the stem a little way with binding tape. Place the next bud so that it lies on top of the stem facing the same way as the first one and the tip of the second one just overlaps the base of the first. Attach in the same way, then continue with the others until all are in position. Arch the stem over backwards so that each bud stands free.

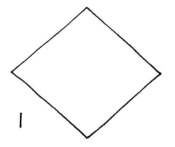

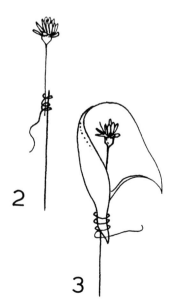

Carnation

Fabric: This tiny little flower can only be made with a very fine fabric like organza.

Shapes: Cut two strips 36cm (14in) by 3cm (1in) with pinking scissors on one side and straight on the other side. Make deep cuts at 1cm (¼in) intervals half way into the strip (Fig 1).

Centre: Thread a tiny bead onto a piece of binding wire and secure to the top of the stem wire (Fig 2).

Petals: Hold the two strips of material together and gather along the entire uncut sides (Fig 3). Roll the material several times around the centre and secure the end of the binding wire.

Stem: Cover the stem with binding tape. This flower has so many petals that the little bead in the centre often disappears from view.

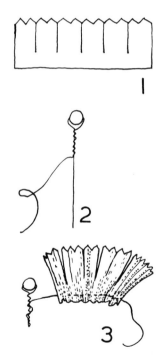

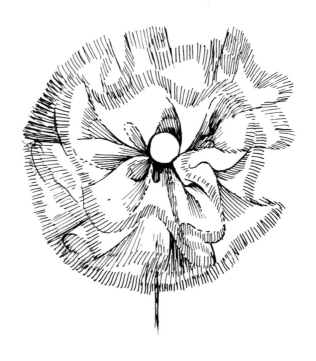

Pom-pom flower

Fabric: The whole filmy effect of the outline of this flower is created by the frayed edge, so choose a loose weave organza which frays easily. The puff ball in the centre serves as a spacer to make the petals stand out.

Shapes: Cut a strip across one yard of material, 5cm (2in) wide.

Centre: Apply glue to the top of a stem wire and push it firmly into the centre of a puff ball and leave it to dry (Fig 1).

Petals: Attach a piece of binding wire to the stem just below the puff ball and gather along the entire length of the fabric (Fig 2). Pull it up as tightly as possible – it will probably encircle the centre twice – and secure the end of the wire to the stem.

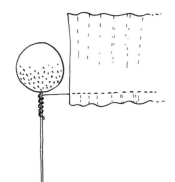

Stem: Cover the stem with binding tape and then fray the edge of your petals until you have a fringe of 1cm ($\frac{1}{4}$in) in depth.

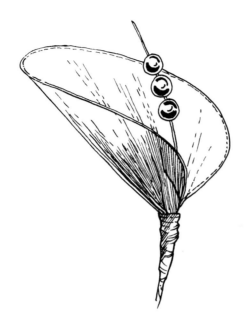

Chiffon arum lily

Fabric: Use chiffon so that the folds in this lily are clearly visible and choose some large round shiny beads for the centre. The petal shape is stretched over a milliners' wire frame.

Shapes: Cut a piece of chiffon 21cm (8in) square and a piece of milliners' wire 33cm (13in) long. Fold the piece of chiffon in half diagonally to form a triangular shape (Fig 1). Place the milliners' wire inside the fold and bring the two ends together, gathering in the raw edges of the chiffon as you do so (Fig 2). Holding the chiffon firmly with one hand, gently push the ends of the wire so that the shape enlarges and the material becomes taut. You will find that as the material tightens the petal forms itself into a coil. Secure this shape with binding wire (Fig 3).

Centre: Use a covered stem wire, apply glue to the top 4cm (1½in) and thread on three large round beads, allowing 1cm (½in) to protrude at the top (Fig 4).

Petals: Hold the binding wire and the centre to the point where the petal shape is bound, and bind everything together firmly with binding wire (Fig 5).

Stem: Cover the base of the petal and the stem with binding tape.

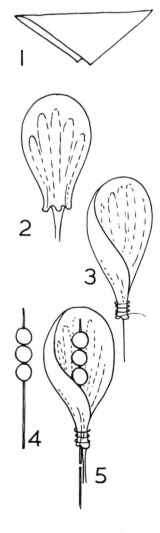

Daisy

Fabric: Use a stiff cotton organdie or even tarlatan if you can find one which is closely woven. Dip the fabric into a gelatine solution.

Shapes: Cut three discs 10cm (4in) wide and make twelve deep cuts to within 2cm ($\frac{1}{2}$in) of the centre (Fig 1). Trim the tip of each petal to a point and mark with a felt tip pen in a contrasting colour (Fig 2). Then, using No 82 flower iron, press a cup shape into the centre of each disc (Fig 3). Turn the discs over and make a trough in the centre of each petal (Fig 4) with iron No 42.

Centre: Use a raffia berry as the centre and join it to the top of a stem wire with binding wire.

Petals: Make a hole in the centre of each petal disc and thread them onto the stem wire, placing them if possible so that the petals are staggered and do not lie directly one above the other.

Stem: Cover the stem with binding tape, several times at the top, in fact enough to hold the petals in place, before you complete the stem.

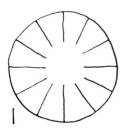

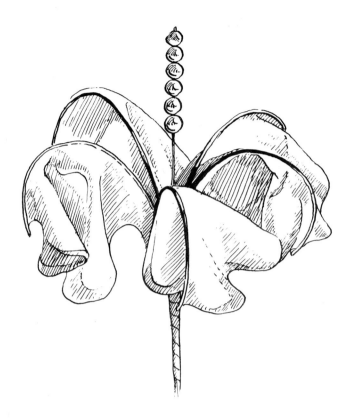

Draped chiffon flower

Fabric: The petals in this flower are draped over a wire frame and float below their support, so chiffon is the ideal material to choose.

Shapes: Cut five fat pointed oval shapes 14cm (5½in) long and 14cm (5½in) wide (Fig 1). Using six pieces of covered stem wire 17cm (6¾in) long, apply glue all round on the top 14cm (5½in), then stick one to the centre of each petal and fold the petal in half over the wire.

Centre: Use six large pearls, thread them onto a covered stem wire and secure their position with glue. Allowing a stem below the beads of 6cm (2½in), and bind it to the top of a stem wire with binding wire.

Petals: Place one beside the centre with fold nearest the beads and bind tightly with binding wire. Repeat the process with the remaining petals arranging them evenly around the centre.

Stem: Cover the base of the petals and the stem with binding tape. Then shape the petals by curving them outwards half way up, and up a little at their tips. The amount of curve you make will depend on your material which should appear to float free of the wires and folds.

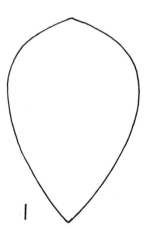

1

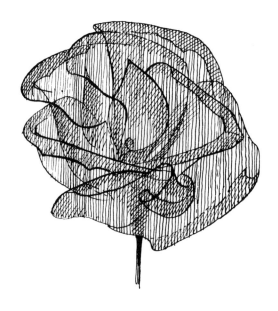

Organdie rose

Fabric: The title suggests the fabric to choose for this rose. Organdie, particularly when cut on the cross, has the quality of being easily moulded with a scissor blade. Consequently a light filmy rose results and this, when dipped into a fabric dye on completion, can give the flower a faint blush.

Shapes: Cut eight pointed rose petal shapes 10cm (4in) long and 7cm (2¾in) wide and cut on the cross (Fig 1). Curl across the top of either side of each petal by pulling the fabric through between your thumb and scissor blade. Start with the first few petals with only a little curve and increase the amount of curve as you progress.

Centre: Curl up the first petal into a tube and bind it tightly to the top of a stem wire.

Petals: Join the next petal by curling it round the centre and continue in that way with the other petals. Each petal should overlap half of the previous one and as you progress gather the base of each petal as you attach it to give a fullness to the centre of the flower.

Stem: Cover the base of the petals and the stem with binding tape. You can vary the size of the roses for flower arrangements by simply using less or more petals. The size can always be varied too but the limit of the largest size will be controlled by the strength of the organdie.

Variation: If this flower is made out of silk the batik method of dyeing can be used to create interestingly patterned petals.

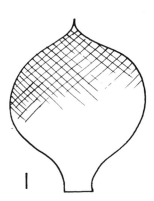

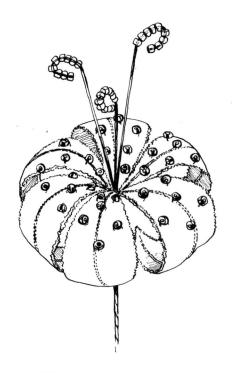

Organdie tiger lily

Fabric: This flower requires a lot of patience in sewing the beads to the petals because, to avoid unsightly lines of cotton joining the dots, they all have to be individually finished. The transparent organdie allows the spots to be seen on both sides of the petals.

Shapes: Cut twelve pointed oval shapes 10cm (4in) long (Fig 1). Sew glass beads at random on half of them to create the spots (Fig 2). Little glass beads are the best to use and they should be as small as possible. Cut six pieces of covered stem wire 12cm (5in) long. Apply glue to the wire all round – not the petals to avoid marking the delicate surface – before placing one on the back of each spotted petal. Then put a plain one on each of the backs, sandwiching the wires in the centre.

Centre: Using the same beads, thread nine onto each of three covered stem wires. Secure their position with glue and bend the tops over to form loops. Then join them together in a bunch and bind to the top of a stem wire with binding wire (Fig 3).

Petals: Place the first petal, spots inward, beside the centre and secure it with binding wire. Attach the others in the same way, spacing them evenly around the stem (Fig 4).

Stem: Cover the base of the petals and stem with binding tape. Then shape the petals by curling first the tips outwards, and continuing with small movements until they are entirely curled back and the centre springs out of the middle. Finally bend the stem until the whole flower head points diagonally downwards.

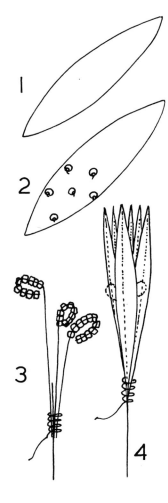

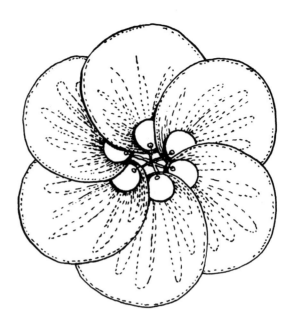

Wired disc flower

Fabric: You will require thin transparent fabric which can still be seen through in spite of the double layer and the gathering at the base of the petals. Chiffon, crepe or nylon tulle would all be satisfactory.

Shapes: Cut six pointed oval shapes 24cm (9½in) long and 14cm (5½in) wide (Fig 1). Fold one of the pieces in half holding a piece of covered stem wire in the fold. Thread a needle with some binding wire and join the end to one end of the milliners' wire. Gather along the edges together and pull it tight drawing the ends of the wire together (Fig 2). Bind the wires together with the binding wire.

Centre: Thread six large flat sequins individually onto stems of binding wire and twist the ends back on themselves to secure the position of the sequins. Thread one through the gathered part of one of the petals and twist the end of the wire round the petal stem (Fig 3). Repeat this with the other sequins.

Petals: Bend the stem of each petal back a little. Arrange them into a bunch with the sequins on the top surface and bind them to the top of a stem wire.

Stem: Cover the base of the petals and the stem with binding tape. Any adjustment required should be made when the flower is complete to make the petals radiate evenly.

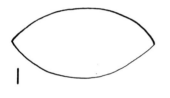

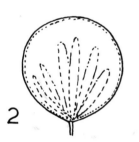

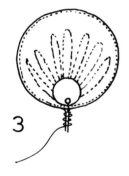

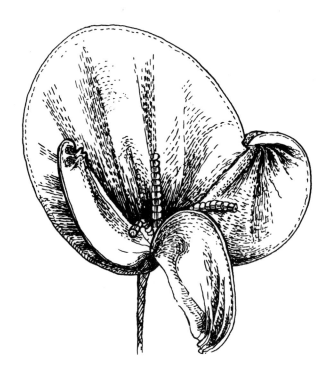

Pansy

Fabric: This is another flower which is gathered around a wire frame, so choose a chiffon, tulle or crepe for the pansy.

Shapes: Cut four pointed oval pieces, one 35cm (14in) long and 23cm (9in) wide and the other three 16cm (6½in) long and 12cm (4½in) wide (Fig 1). Fold the largest in half lengthways with a covered stem wire in the fold. Thread a needle with binding wire and join the end to one of the ends of the milliners' wire. Gather the two loose edges together and pull it very tight until they meet and form a looped frame. Twist the ends together and finish off the gathering with binding wire. Treat the other petals in the same way, but instead of pulling the gathering up tight, pull it until the gathering bends the wire and the petal is crescent shaped, (Fig 2).

Centre: Make three stems of eleven little glass beads, arrange them in a bunch and attach them to the top of a stem wire.

Petals: Arrange the three crescent petals so that the centre one points up with one on either side pointing downwards (Fig 3). Bind this bunch around the centre of a binding wire, then place the large round petal behind the others and bind this on too.

Stem: Cover the base of the petals and stem with binding tape, adding extra ones as you do so if more support is necessary. Separate the petals and bend the stem so that the flower faces forward.

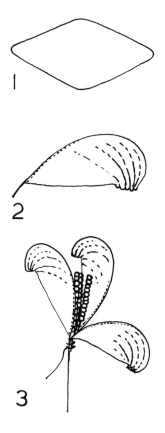

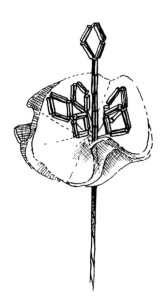

Little frilly flower

Fabric: Use tarlatan or net for this little flower to achieve the powder puff effect of the finished petals.

Shapes: Cut three discs 3cm (1¼in) in diameter (Fig 1).

Centre: To contrast with the very simple petal shapes, a complicated assembly of stamens is built up in the centre. Thread four bugle beads onto each of five pieces of binding wire before twisting the ends back and forming loops (Fig 2). Then thread on one of them five more beads for the stem. Bunch them together and bind them to the top of a stem wire with binding wire.

Petals: Push the stem wire through the centre of all the little discs and bind them to the stem so that they gather themselves slightly.

Stem: Cover the base of the petals and the stem with binding tape. Separate the layers so that the flower is entirely frilly.

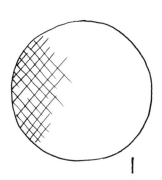

67

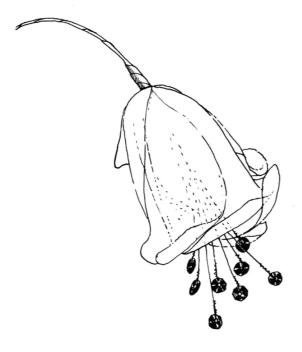

Harebell

Fabric: Use organdie for this delicate flower so that the petals can be moulded into shape.

Shapes: Cut six round petal shapes 6cm (2½in) in diameter with a little stem shape 2cm (¾in) long (Fig 1). Use a No 42 flower iron and make a trough across the top of each one.

Centre: Use eight little sequins and thread each one individually onto a stem of binding wire and twist the ends back on themselves so as to secure the sequin. Make them into a bunch of varying lengths and bind them to the top of a stem wire with binding wire.

Petals: Coil the first petal round the centre and bind it into position with binding wire. Continue in this way with the other petals overlapping each one by half.

Stem: Cover the base of the petals and stem with binding tape. Arch the top of the stem over until the harebell hangs down.

Colour Plate 5
All the flowers are made with remnants bought at a furnishing fabric sale and are consequently rather heavy, but there are several subtle shades of brown and yellow. Their centres are made with various types of seeds which combine happily with the quality of the petals. The areas between the flowers are filled with dried allium seeds.

Colour Plate 6
Using this miniature liqueur
bottle, the complete
arrangement measures only
21cm (8in) high and the little
carnations have glass drop
beads in the centre which
match exactly the colour
of the bottle. The little
leaf shapes are simply
threaded glass beads looped
onto a stem wire.

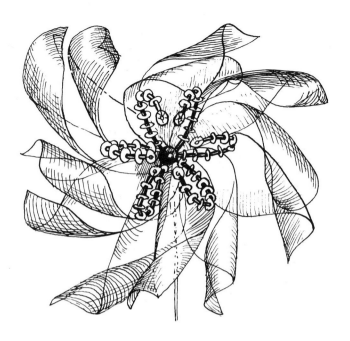

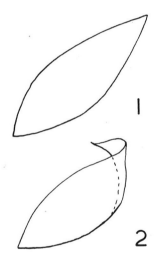

Twisted flower

Fabric: Use organdie for this flower because not only are the petals moulded but this is a comparatively large flower which can be used for small arrangements and therefore should appear as delicate as possible.

Shapes: Cut twelve pointed oval shapes 10cm ($3\frac{3}{4}$in) long and 3cm ($1\frac{1}{4}$in) wide (Fig 1). Notice that they should be cut on the cross. Curl diagonally the right hand top side of each petal by drawing the petal between your thumb and a scissor blade (Fig 2).

Centre: Thread one pearl bead onto a piece of binding wire and attach it to the stem. Thread eight beads and sequins alternately onto six stems of binding wire, twisting the end back on itself round the first sequins before threading the lower ones. Secure the position of the last beads with a little glue. Arrange them in a bunch of the bead part only, leaving no wire stem showing around the pearl, and bind them to the top of a stem wire with binding wire. Shape each stamen into a loop (Fig 3).

Petals: Place the petals individually curling outwards around the centre and bind them tightly. You should make one circle of half of the petals with the remaining half in the spaces behind them.

Stem: Bind the base of the petals and the stem with binding tape.

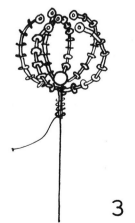

71

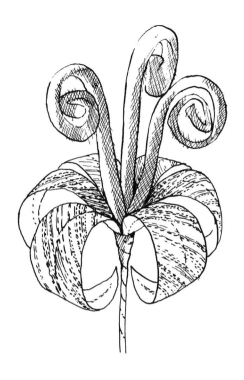

Fantasy flower

Fabric: You will need organdie for the tendrils in the centre and silk, satin or taffeta for the petals which are lined with iron-on vilene.

Shapes: Cut six identical pointed oval shapes 17cm (7in) long and 5cm (2in) wide from both the silk and the vilene, making twelve altogether (Fig 1). Use six lengths of covered binding wire and press the petals together, layers of silk and vilene, the wire in the centre, with an iron (Fig 2).

Centre: Cut three strips of organdie 22cm (9in) long by 7cm (3in) wide, cut on the cross (Fig 3). Hold one at tension on your knee and roll it many times until the tube holds its shape, and repeat with the other two. Thread a stem wire up the centre of each tube. Make the three into a bunch and bind it tightly to the top of a stem wire with binding tape.

Petals: Hold one of the petals, silk side inwards, and bind it to the centre and repeat the process with the remaining five.

Stem: Cover the base of the petals and the stem with binding tape, adding extra stem wires if necessary. Curl the petals, tips first, in small movements until they are curled right back. Then shape the stamens by bending each one out a little, then up straight, before making a curl outwards at the top.

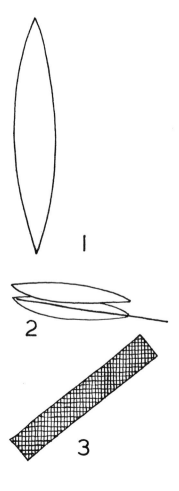

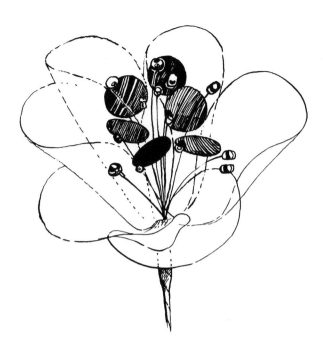

Organdie cup

Fabric: Either white or coloured organdie forms the simple matt surface on the petals which contrasts with the shiny beads and sequins in the centre.

Shapes: Cut six simple round petal shapes 6cm (2½in) diameter with a short stem, (Fig 1).

Centre: Thread seven little glass beads individually onto its own stem of binding wire and twist the ends back on themselves to secure the position of the beads (Fig 2). Use six big flat sequins, and to each add 2 more small beads, one each side (Fig 3) and put them onto wire stems in the same way. Bunch them all together and bind them to the top of a stem wire (Fig 4).

Petals: Make a pleat at the stem of one petal and bind it to the centre, then add the others in the same way arranging them evenly round the stem.

Stem: Cover the base of the petals and stem with binding tape. This flower shape is also effective made with two layers of silk combined with iron-on vilene.

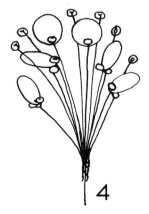

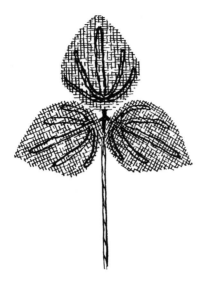

Trillium

Fabric: This is a tiny little flower so really organdie is the best fabric to choose. It is also a good surface for the stitching on the petals.

Shapes: Cut three droplet-shaped petals 2½cm (1in) long (Fig 1). Thread a contrast colour in your sewing machine and sew vein lines onto the petals echoing the outline of the petal, and one straight up the centre (Fig 2). Glue a short length of stem wire to the back of each petal (Fig 3).

Petals: Bind the stem of each petal to the main stem and arrange them evenly.

Stem: Cover the base of the petals and the stem with binding tape. Press the petals out so that the little flower is flat.

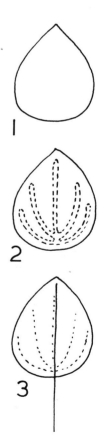

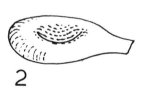

Crinkle poppy

Fabric: The crinkles in this poppy are in the crepe chiffon already and form an interesting texture. The fabric is naturally too flimsy to hold the petal shape, so first dip your fabric into a gelatine solution but do not iron it as it dries.

Petals: Cut ten rounded petal shapes 4cm (1½in) diameter (Fig 1) and one 7cm (3in) long pointed oval shape for the centre. Shape the round petals by making a cup in the centre of each with No 82 flower iron. Then turn them over to make troughs along the tops with No 42 flower iron (Fig 2).

Centre: Join a piece of binding wire to the top of a stem wire. Fold the oval piece in half and then cross one side over the other (Fig 3). Bind this bud shape to the stem.

Petals: Bind each petal separately to the stem, making each one overlap the previous one by half.

Stem: Cover the base of the petals and stem with binding tape. If the petals tumble, simply allow them to settle in their natural position.

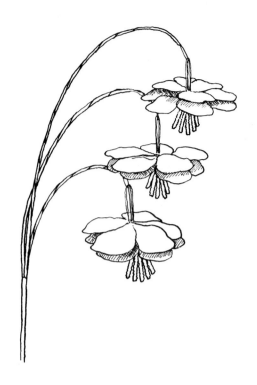

Swinging flowers

Fabric: These little frilly flowers have been made with stiffened organdie, but fine silk or taffeta would be equally successful. Whichever fabric you choose, dip it in a gelatine solution before you start. This is a delicate little flower so do not choose a fabric which would make the flowers cumbersome.

Shapes: Cut two discs 5cm (2in) wide and then trim the edges to create five petal shapes (Fig 1). Use a No 82 flower iron and press a hollow in the centre of each flower.

Centre: Use three pairs of ready-made stamens for each flower. Fold each one in half, put binding wire in the folds and twist the ends together (Fig 2).

Petals: Ease the delicate twisted stem through the centre of one of the flowers and bend the ends back into the flower to form a tiny loop. Repeat this with the other two.

Stem: Use a piece of binding wire threaded through the tiny wire loops and bind it to the top of a stem wire (Fig 3). Cover the binding and a little of the stem with binding tape. Repeat the process with the remaining flowers before completing the stem binding. Arch the top of the stem over so that the flowers can hang freely from the stem and each other.

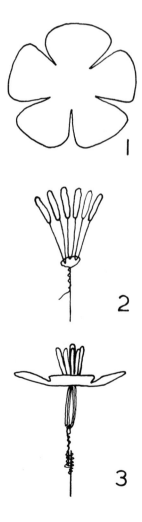

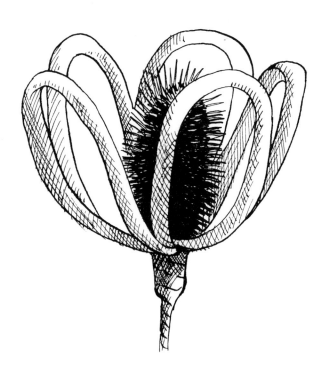

Loop teazle tulip

Fabric: Around the teazle in the centre there are loops of organdie in this fantasy flower.

Shapes: Cut six strips 23cm (9in) long by 11cm (4½in) cut on the cross (Fig 1). Holding one of the strips at tension on your knee, roll it like pastry sufficient times until the roll stays in place. Use six covered stem wires, thread one into each tube and bend it over to form a loop by twisting the ends together (Fig 2). Curve the loop over slightly.

Centre: The teazle fills the centre. If the natural stem has broken you can add a wire stem. Make a loop on the top of a stem wire, place it beside the natural stem and bind the two together.

Petals: Hold one of the petals beside the teazle and bind tightly with binding wire as close under the seed head as possible. As you add the petals arrange them evenly around the teazle.

Stem: Cover the base of the petals and stem with binding tape.

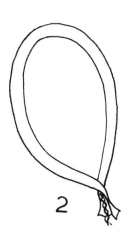

77

Cyclamen

Fabric: The centre is a covered puff ball so choose some shiny silk for this with matching thread and some contrasting coloured net on which to make the stitches.

Shapes: Cut ten round petals, 7cm (2½in) diameter with a slight stalk (Fig 1). Thread your sewing machine with the coloured thread and sew a winding zig-zag onto each petal (Fig 2). Then roll each petal into a funnel shape and secure with binding wire (Fig 3).

Centre: First cover a stem wire, put a little glue on the top, then stick a puff ball onto it and leave to dry. Cut a disc 7cm (2½in) wide, put the puff ball into the centre and gather all the sides in and secure with binding wire as close to the puff ball as possible.

Petals: Bind the first petal to the centre with the fold uppermost. Bind it very tightly so that it will naturally fall away from the centre. Add the others separately so that they are evenly spaced and also fall away from the centre.

Stem: Cover the base of the petals and stem with binding tape. Then bend the stem over so that the flower faces downwards.

Vermicelli lily

Fabric: Use tarlatan for this lily because the stiff texture is required to hold the shape whilst the transparent quality allows the embroidery to dominate the design.

Shapes: Cut one pointed oval shape 11cm (4in) long and 7cm (3in) wide (Fig 1). Put a contrasting colour thread in your sewing machine and make random vermicelli stitches to cover all but the edges of the petal (Fig 2).

Centre: Use three round beads, apply glue to the top of a covered stem wire and thread them onto it and leave to dry (Fig 3).

Petals: Curve the petal shape round and bind it to the stem so that it encircles it once and the beads are seen to lie in the centre of the petal.

Stem: Cover the base of the petals and stem with binding tape.

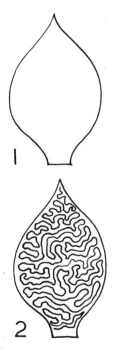

7 Cotton, Hessian, Suede and Felt Flowers

A tall candlestick forms an excellent support for this dramatic arrangement. The heavier material used for the diagonal poppies and hessian trumpets gives a rather severe shape which is relieved by the fronds of barley and butcher's broom in the background (see Colour Plate 3, Page 51).

Hessian tulip

Fabric: Furnishing fabric, hessian in this case, is used to create the rather heavy quality of this flower. Choose two shades which will combine happily.

Shapes: Cut five small rounded shapes 18cm (7in) from one piece of fabric and five larger rounded shapes 26cm (10in) from the other (Fig 1). Apply glue to the edges to prevent fraying.

Centre: First cover a stem wire with binding tape, then stick a styro foam ball on the top with some glue. Cover the entire surface of the ball with glue and dip it into some mixed bird seed until it is completely covered (Fig 2).

Petals: Make a pleat in the base of one of the small petals and bind it to the stem, just below the centre. Continue to add the remaining small petals in the same way (Fig 3). Arrange them evenly round the centre before you add the large ones. All the petals should overlap slightly. Make the pleats big enough to enable the petals to support themselves and keep the outline of the flower cup shaped.

Stem: Cover the base of the petals and the stem with binding tape, adding any further wires required to support the heavy flower head.

Variation: This flower could equally well be made with many of the close weave furnishing fabrics – cottons, hemp or canvas. Also a puff ball is a perfectly good substitute for the styro foam ball.

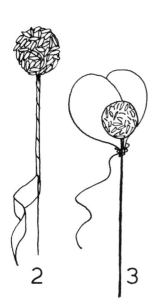

Mob-cap flower

Fabric: This stylised flower lends itself to the use of any pattern-ed cotton or stiff material which will hold its shape in a bell; gingham is particularly suitable. You will need a piece 28cm (11in) by 10cm (4in), and this can be attractively decorated with ric-rac trimming.

Centre: As this is a pendant flower in which the stamens are visible below the bell, a length of knotted cord is most suitable – one length of 31cm (12in) knotted at each end. Fold it to make two uneven lengths and place the stem wire through the fold and twist the end of the wire back on itself (Fig 1).

Petals: Hem along one long side of the material and attach the ric-rac 3cm (1in) in from the edge. Then join the two short ends to form a ring (Fig 2). Gather along the unfinished side to form a skirt (Fig 3). Place it over the stamens and hold it all in place with binding wire.

Stem: Cover the base of the petals and stem with binding tape, then bend the stem over to allow the little mob cap to hang.

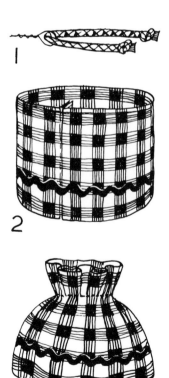

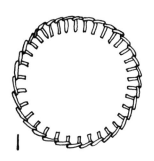

Embroidered hollyhocks

Fabric: Use felt for these flowers to avoid having to make cumbersome hems at the edges of the curved petal shapes. The centres are a tassel form created from a piece of lampshade fringing. Choose some stranded silk for the embroidery around the edges of the petals to match the centre. I made three small flowers initially, but several more would be quite attractive on one stem.

Shapes: Cut three discs 5cm (2in) wide, and embroider blanket stitch evenly all round the edges.

Centre: Cut three strips of lampshade fringing 3cm (1in) long and roll them up like a cigarette. Bind them tightly to the top of three stem wires (Fig 2). Cut off the binding wire at this point.

Petals: Make a small hole in the centre of each petal shape and ease the stem wires through them, pushing them as far up under the centre as possible.

Stem: Bind the stems several times just under the flower heads, until the petals are held in position, before you complete the stem binding. Assemble your three flowers by joining them one above the other to a long wire stem with binding tape. No extra binding wire is required. Finally make each little flower face forwards.

83

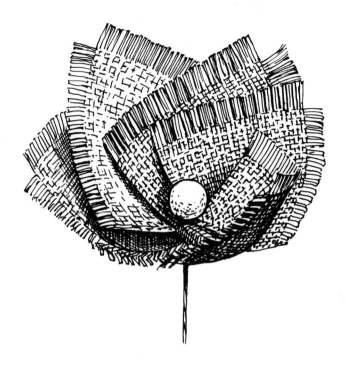

Hessian diagonal poppy

Fabric: Generally hessian is firm enough to support the shape of the petal but if not it can be dipped in a gelatine solution.

Shapes: Cut five petals 8cm (3in) square and pull four strands from two adjoining sides, sealing the edges with glue (Fig 1).

Centre: Cover a stem wire with binding tape and secure a puff ball to the top with glue (Fig 2).

Petals: Make a pleat in the unfrayed corner of one of the petals and bind it to the stem just below the puff ball. Then add the remaining petals separately in the same way. Arrange them evenly round the centre and ensure that each one overlaps the next.

Stem: Cover the base of the petals and the stem with binding tape, adding additional stem wires if necessary to support the heavy flower head. If the petals fall open apply a little glue at the point where they overlap.

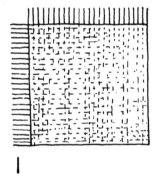

1

2

Hessian clematis

Fabric: Hessian has been chosen for this flower because the large petals are supported by a central wire only.

Shapes: Cut six long thin pointed shapes 15cm (6in) long and 5cm (2in) wide (Fig 1). Use covered wire and cut eight pieces 16cm (6¼in) long and glue one to the back of each petal (Fig 2).

Centre: Sunflower seeds are used for the stamens. Use covered stem wire and cut twelve pieces 10cm (4in) long. Carefully make a hole in the thick part of twelve seeds and push one onto the top of each wire and secure with glue (Fig 3). Assemble them into a bunch, all the same length, and bind them to the top of a stem wire.

Petals: Bind the wire stem of each petal to the centre, arranging them evenly and keeping the wire backing the petals on the inside (Fig 4).

Stem: Cut off all the spare covered wired that is below the binding. Cover the stem with binding tape. Finally shape the petals out at the base, in towards the centre, then curl the tips outwards again; this will leave space to separate the stamens.

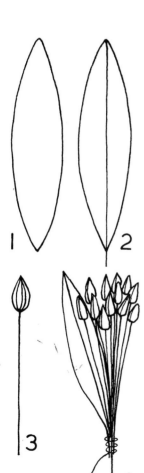

85

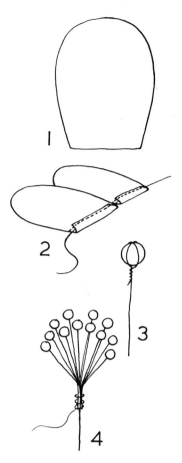

Cotton floppy poppy

Fabric: Generally patterned fabrics, particularly bold ones, look unsatisfactory as flowers because the pattern tends to overwhelm the design. In this case however a small overall pattern, flowered or otherwise, can give a summery quality to these cotton poppies.

Shapes: Cut six oval shapes 10cm (4in) long and 8cm (3in) wide (Fig 1). Fold the base of each petal over and machine them in a line, holding a piece of binding wire in the fold (Fig 2).

Centre: Use some round seeds for the centre and make a tiny 'cage' for each one with a twist of binding wire, the ends of which, when twisted together, hold the seed in place (Fig 3). Make a bunch of twelve of these clustered together and bind them to the top of a stem wire (Fig 4).

Petals: Gather the length of petals up tightly, and bind it to the stem just below the centre so that they encircle it once.

Stem: Cover the base of the petals and stem with binding tape.

Colour Plate 7
The basket plaque on which this spray is made comes from Tuscany. The five grapes are covered with donkey brown velvet and the five tiny salmon coloured silk rose buds are intermingled with dried plant material. There is a fir cone in the centre with some helichrysum, butcher's broom and harestail grasses. The solidity of the cluster is relieved by bunches of glyxia and some quaking grass.

Colour Plate 8
The line of five various sized
Thomas's flowers, are the
only fabric flowers in
this design. Together with
ferns and other dried plant
materials they sit on a
piece of olive wood.

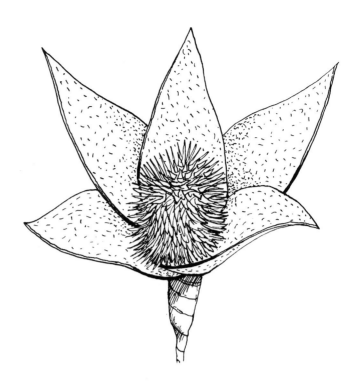

Suede teazle flower

Fabric: The suede has a strange quality in being substantial enough to support the petal shapes and yet slightly flexible so that it can be stretched over the seed head.

Shapes: Cut five pointed oval shapes 14cm (5½in) long and 6cm (2¼in) wide (Fig 1).

Centre: The teazle forms the centre and may need the addition of a wire stem for support.

Petals: Make a small pleat at the end of one petal before binding it closely to the base of the teazle with the rough side of the suede inside. Then repeat the process with the remaining five, spacing them evenly round the teazle.

Stem: Cover the stem with binding tape and then pull the tip of each petal until it stands upright. The prickles in the teazle will hold it in place.

1

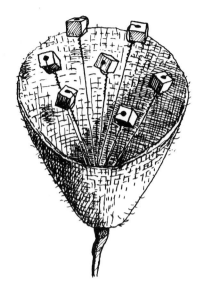

Hessian trumpet

Fabric: The heavy weave in hessian makes an interesting pattern on this rather severe little flower. Hessian woven in two colours is the best to use.

Shapes: Cut out one fan shaped piece of hessian 12cm (5in) diameter and apply glue all along the outside edge to prevent fraying. Then curl the whole shape round and glue the edges together to form the trumpet (Fig 1).

Centre: Use seven little square wooden beads and thread each one onto binding wire and twist the ends back to hold the beads in place. Make them into a bunch, all the same length, and bind onto a stem wire.

Petals: Thread the stem through the centre of the trumpet and hold in place with the binding wire.

Stem: Cover the base of the petals and the stem with binding tape. Separate the beads so that they fill the area in the trumpet.

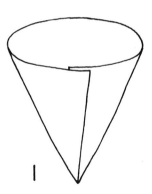

1

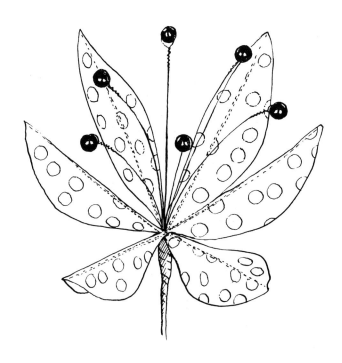

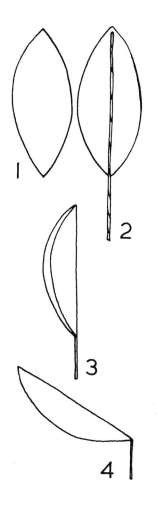

Spotty flower

Fabric: A light translucent cotton with a woven spot rather than a printed one is the quality required for this flower. Also try to find fabric that resists fraying as this will save having to glue all the edges.

Shapes: Cut six pointed oval shapes 10cm (4in) long and 4cm (1½in) wide (Fig 1). Cover eight pieces of stem wire 14cm (5½in) long with binding tape and glue one to the centre of each petal (Fig 2). Fold each one over along the wire (Fig 3).

Centre: Use six little round shiny beads, thread each one onto a piece of binding wire and secure them in place by twisting the ends of the wire together. Arrange them into a bunch with 10cm (4in) stems and bind them to the top of a stem wire.

Petals: Bend the stem of each petal back a little (Fig 4), and bind each one separately to the centre at the same point as the stamens. Arrange them evenly around the centre.

Stem: Cover the base of the petals and stem with binding tape. Space the stamens out so that they fill the area within the circle of petals.

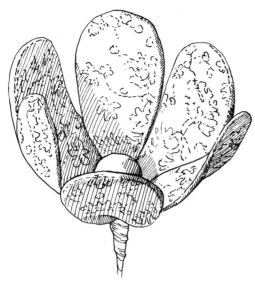

Wired cotton poppy

Fabric: The wire frame supports the weight, from the thinnest fabric to heavy cottons or indeed velvet, but avoid bulky materials. This method is particularly suitable for embroidered petals as they are lined by the second layer of material.

Shapes: Cut twelve petal shapes 10cm (4in) long, 7cm (3in) at widest point (Fig 1), and place them together in pairs, inside out, and machine them together all round the edge. Ease them out the right way and push a length of milliners' wire inside to form the frame. Push as much wire in as possible, in fact, until the fabric is taut and the whole shape curves over in tension (Fig 2). Twist the ends of the wire together and sew the unfinished ends to the base of the frame holding the fabric in tension.

Centre: Use a puff ball for the centre. First cover a stem wire with binding tape before glueing the ball on the top. Then cut a circular piece of cotton 7cm (3in) diameter and machine all round the edge with the tension adjusted so that the stitching can be gathered (Fig 3). Put the disc over the puff ball and pull the stitching up as tightly as possible and hold it in place with binding wire.

Petals: Ease the stem of each petal shape slightly (Fig 4). Bind each one into place around the centre allowing the petals to curve inwards over the centre.

Stem: Cover the base of the petals and stem with binding tape. If the wire fails to support the heavy stem you will need to add extra stem wires and bind them with the original one.

Variation: Any number of petals can be used for this flower. The curve of the petals could also be varied which would result in a type of iris. Enormous stylised flowers can be made from this pattern, together with enormous green leaves.

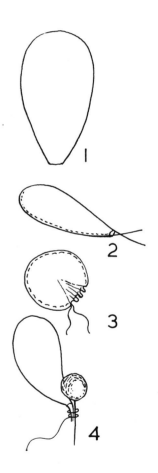

8 Leaves Berries and Seeds

These are a combination of fabric fruit and berries, glass fruit and vegetables, and vine leaves made of hessian bonded card, normally used for lampshade making. They are a simple leaf shape with a stem wire glued on the reverse side. The ribbon is allowed to tumble out over the side of the pedestal.

Spiral bulrush

Fabric: Rolled organdie is used for the spiral bulrush. As the pieces are cut on the cross this can be an opportunity for using any odd scraps.

Shapes: Cut a piece 104cm (41in) long diagonally on the cross 6cm (2½in) wide. Place the strip on your knee and, pulling the piece in tension, roll it in several places until the organdie remains rolled.

Assembly: Thread your longest piece of stem wire through the centre of the roll (Fig 1) and shape into a spiral.

Stem: Join the end of the wire to another stem wire. Cover the join and the stem with binding tape. You will find that you have a springy bulrush which creates its own natural curve.

Couched leaf

Fabric: Use silk or heavy satin for this leaf, which is strengthened by making two layers and sandwiching bondina in the middle.

Shapes: Cut two rectangular shapes from the material and one from the bondina 13cm (5in) by 5cm (2in). Sandwich the bondina in the centre of the two fabrics, shiny sides outwards

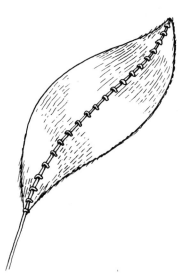

and press them together with a warm iron. Cut a pointed oval shape from the piece (Fig 1).

Assembly: Cut a piece of covered stem wire 18cm (7in) long. Hold it on top of the leaf shape and embroider couching stitches along its length.

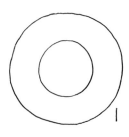

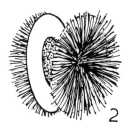

Woolly ball leonotis

Fabric: This traditional woolly ball's close similarity to a leonotis allows its inclusion in a flower-making book. The materials needed are wool and card.

Shapes: Cut two discs of card 8cm (3in) in diameter and cut a hole in the centre 1cm ($\frac{1}{2}$in) in diameter (Fig 1). Place the two together and bind the wool round and round until the hole in the centre is full. Holding the centre firmly cut all the loops around the outside edge, and ease the pieces of card apart a little (Fig 2). Insert a double piece of wool between the pieces of card and tie it as tightly as possible, as this holds the whole ball together. Finally, cut away the pieces of card. You may find it necessary to trim the edges of the wool as you ease it into a ball shape.

Bulrush

Fabric: Velvet is naturally the material to use because the texture of the fabric so closely resembles the real thing.

Shapes: Cut a piece of velvet 11cm (4in) square and fold it in half with the right side inside. Sew along one short side and the long one to make a bag (Fig 1).

Assembly: Turn the shape inside out. Cover a stem wire and push it into and right through the end of the bag until it protrudes 3cm (1in) (Fig 2). Stuff the bag with kapok evenly around the stem until it is a cylindrical shape.

Stem: Cover the base of the bulrush and the stem with binding tape.

Variations: Satin is an alternative material to use; whilst not so realistic, it does have a shiny quality which is shown to advantage on the bulrush.

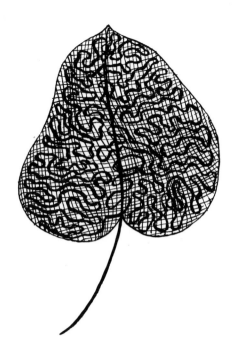

Vermicelli leaf

Fabric: This leaf is made on a double layer of tarlatan so that, whilst being transparent, it will support its own weight.

Shapes: Cut two heart shaped pieces 8cm (3in) long and 6cm (2½in) wide (Fig 1). Put a contrasting colour cotton in your sewing machine and make a vermicelli pattern on the double fabric, stitching at random the entire surface, taking care not to cross any other lines (Fig 2).

Assembly: Apply glue to the top half of a 16cm (6½in) length of covered stem wire and stick it to the centre of the back of the leaf.

Stem: It already has a short stem which requires no covering, but if you wish to attach a long one, the two will require a covering of binding tape. Curve the whole leaf shape over gently.

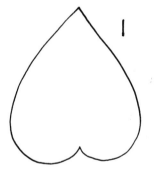

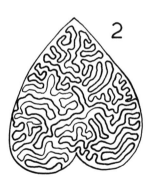

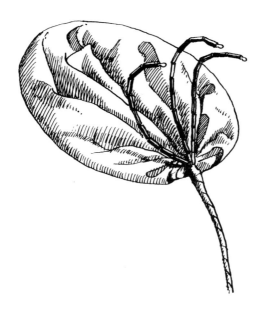

Silk disc leaf

Fabric: Silk, a fine lawn or even tulle would make a successful disc leaf. Then choose some little glass beads to blend with the fabric.

Shapes: Cut a pointed oval shape 26cm (10in) long by 12cm (5in) wide (Fig 1). Fold it in half lengthways and place a piece of milliners' wire in the fold before you gather the free sides, both at the same time (Fig 2). Pull the gathering up until the two wires touch and can be bound together. Cut three lengths of binding wire 6cm (2½in) long. Thread a bead onto one and secure by twisting the end back on itself (Fig 3) before adding nine more. Repeat the process with the other two stems and bind the three together in a bunch.

Assembly: Join the bunch of bead stems to the top of a stem wire with binding wire. Thread the stem through the gathering in the disc leaf and secure into position with the same binding wire.

Stem: Cover the stem with binding tape. Curve the beads until they stand freely above the leaf like curved feelers. Bend the leaf backwards a little; the amount you bend it will depend where you intend to place it in your arrangement, because it should be horizontal.

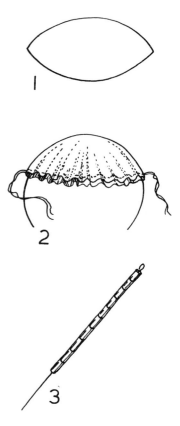

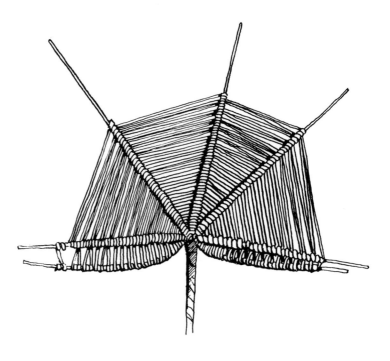

Webbed leaf

Fabric: The idea for this leaf came from those toy tables and other furniture made with pins, conkers and wool. For this leaf, wire replaces the pins and wool or other types of thread can be used to bind round them.

Shapes: Cut seven pieces of covered stem wire 14cm (5½in) long. Bind them together in a bunch, then fan them out (Fig 1).

Assembly: Join the end of the wool to the stem, wind it round one of the wires (Fig 2). Work right across the wires, winding the wool round each one in turn. At the end, turn the fan over and work back again. Continue in this way until the entire surface is covered. Be careful to keep even tension during the manufacture to avoid parts of the leaf sagging. Tie a knot at the end and tuck the ends in.

Stem: Cover the stem with binding tape.

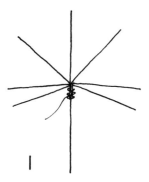

1

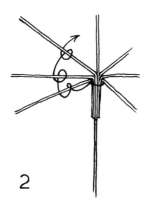

2

Raffia butcher's broom

Fabric: Use coloured raffia, in particular the mossy green shade which makes the most realistic leaves, but of course this can be varied to fit in with your colour scheme.

Shapes: Cut nine pieces 5cm (2in) long and flatten out the wrinkles. Make a double twist in the centre of each one (Fig 1). Fold the piece in half at the twist and join the ends by twisting them both together (Fig 2).

Stem: Join one to the top of a stem wire and bind a little way down with binding tape. Then place a pair at once on each side of the stem and attach it to the stem in the same way. Then, finally, the last pair before completing the stem binding.

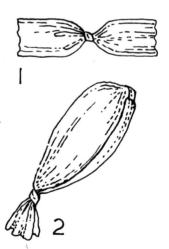

1

2

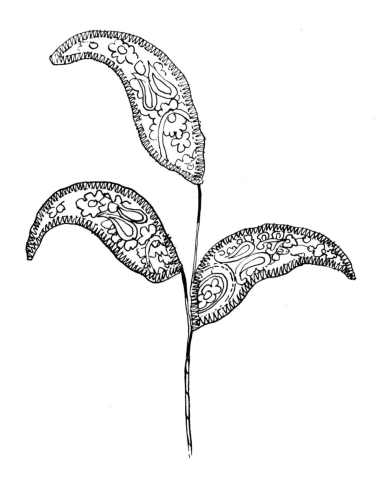

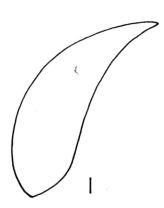

Paisley leaf spray

Fabric: It is the beautiful curved shape of the paisley design that produces this particular leaf, so chose any fabric provided it has the paisley leaf pattern.

Shapes: Cut out five rough shapes to allow extra material around each paisley shape (Fig 1).

Assembly: Shape a piece of bound stem wire as near as possible to the leaf shape, then sew all round the edge using the zig-zag attachment on the machine, encasing the wire within the stitches. Cut away any surplus material, but leave enough free wire for a tiny stem. Repeat the process with four more.

Stem: Join one leaf to the top of a stem wire and bind it for a little way with binding tape, then add another and so on until all are assembled. Cover the remaining stem.

101

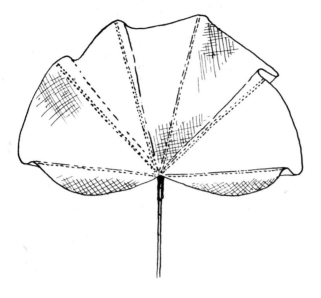

Lady's mantle

Fabric: The finest silk or slightly transparent fabric like organdie, chiffon or loose weave material is required to produce a light filmy effect, plus some iron-on vilene interlining. As the leaf should drape; the vilene should be as fine as possible.

Shapes: Cut a disc shape 15cm (6in) diameter from both the vilene and the top fabric.

Assembly: Cut six pieces of covered stem wire 10cm (4in) long, bind them together in a bunch before fanning them out to radiate from the stem (Fig 1). Place the top fabric face down on the ironing board, then the wires with the stem in the centre (Fig 2). Cut into the centre from the edge of the vilene and place it on top of the rest (Fig 3). Press hard with the iron until all the layers stay together. Enlarge the cut through both layers and curve the sides. Trim the edge with scissors and cover the stem with binding tape. Finally ease the wires together until the fabric drapes between the wires.

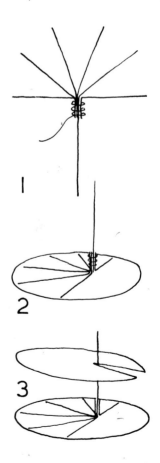

1

2

3

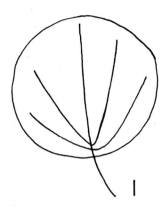

Net ivy leaf

Fabric: Net or any open-weave fabric can be used for these leaves as they are pressed onto iron-on vilene.

Assembly: Use three pieces of covered stem wire, two 15cm (6in) and the other 20cm (8in) long. Cut one disc of vilene 10cm (4in) diameter and one of net. Lie the vilene down on an ironing board, sticky side up, and put the longest wire in the centre. Bend the two other wires in half and open them out again and place the folds on the central wire to create a fan shape (Fig 1). Then place the net on top and press firmly with an iron. Shape the ivy leaf around the wire shape (Fig 2). Join the protruding wire to a stem wire and cover it with binding tape.

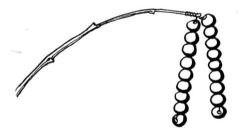

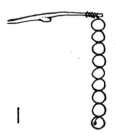

Bead catkins

Fabric: Round beads are the best, and a branch of wood on which to hang the catkins is needed.

Assembly: Thread one bead onto a piece of binding wire and twist the end back on itself to secure it, before adding eight more. Bind the free wire at the top of one of the branches (Fig 1). If this is done very neatly there should be no need for stem binding to cover it. Then repeat the process until every tip has at least one catkin hanging from it.

Spring leaf

Fabric: You will need some crochet string and a length of expansion spring.

Shapes: Cut an 18cm (7in) piece of spring and join the two ends together, by entwining one within the other, to form a loop (Fig 1). Cover a stem wire and push it as far as possible through the centre of the spring until it supports the shape firmly.

Assembly: Join the end of the crochet string with binding wire to the stem and work around the spring catching every third or fourth loop from alternate sides of the stem working an ever increasing cross (Fig 2).

Stem: Cover the ends of the string, together with the stem, with binding tape. For a Christmas decoration this would be effective using gold thread.

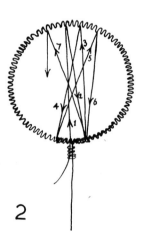

Bead alder

Fabric: Use small round beads and a small branch of wood; if you can find alder this would naturally be the best.

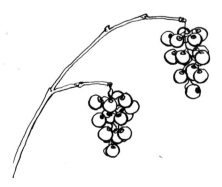

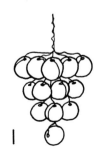

Assembly: Thread thirteen beads separately onto thirteen small pieces of binding wire and secure their position by twisting the ends back on themselves. Arrange them into a bunch with one at the top, then a circle of three, then one of four and the last of five, all one above the other (Fig 1) to make a bunch resembling a blackberry. Join the little bunch to the tip of one of the twigs so that it hangs down, then add as many more as you require.

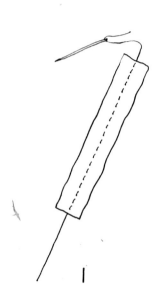

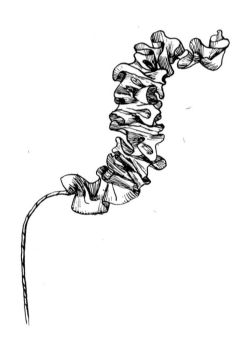

Ribbon fern

Fabric: The width of ribbon used can vary enormously but choose a soft ribbon of satin, nylon or even velvet, and not petersham or the corded type.

Shapes: If you are using a 2·5cm (1in) wide ribbon, then cut a piece 40cm (16in) long.

Assembly: Thread a needle with binding wire and gather the entire length of the ribbon (Fig 1). The wire you choose should be strong enough to support the ribbon; double it up if necessary. Then attach the remaining wire to the top of a stem wire.

Stem: Cover the stem with binding tape and then bend the fern into the required shape.

Bead tendril

Fabric: Little glass beads are effective and the size can be chosen to suit your requirements.

Assembly: Thread about 40 beads onto a stem wire, securing the top and bottom one with glue (Fig 1).

Stem: Cover the remaining stem with binding tape. Twist the beaded part round a pencil, then withdraw it to leave the spiral.

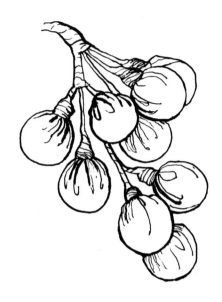

Grapes

Fabric: A shiny material like silk should be used to create highlights on the grapes.

Assembly: Use puff balls for the shape of the grapes and cut nine discs 10cm (4in) diameter. First cover all stems with tape and glue a puff ball on the top of each one. Gather all round the edge of one disc, place it over a puff ball (Fig 1), pull the gathering up tight and secure with binding wire. Cut away any surplus material before covering it and the stem with more tape. Repeat the process with all the others. Then assemble the bunch by twisting one to the top of a stem wire and cover 5cm (2in) of stem, then join two at the next point, and then continue in threes until all are used up and the bunch is arranged evenly.

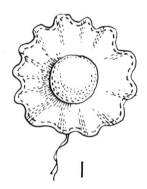

Raffia berry

Fabric: This little berry can also be used for a centre in the flowers. The actual size depends on the size of the puff ball on which it is made. Raffia is used because it can be flattened on the outside and should be used wet so that it is slightly stretchy.

Assembly: Join a puff ball to a stem wire by pushing the wire right through it like a bead and twisting the end of the wire back on itself. Hold the end of the raffia inside the wire twist (Fig 1). Then cover the surface by binding it very tightly, so that the raffia lies flat on the surface. Gradually work round the ball until it is evenly covered.

Stem: Cover the stem with the same material.

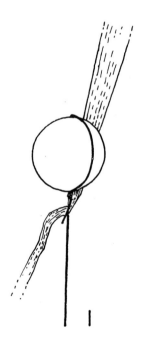

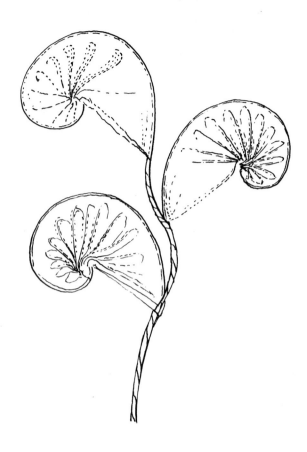

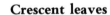

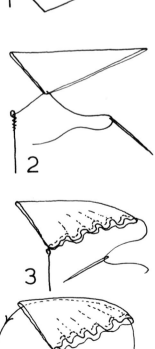

Crescent leaves

Fabric: Use chiffon or a transparent material so that it is possible to see the layers of gathers when the leaves are complete.

Shapes: Cut three kite-shaped pieces 27cm (11in) long and 12cm (5in) wide (Fig 1).

Assembly: Fold one piece in half. Make a hook on the top of a stem wire, attach a piece of milliners' wire to this and thread the wire into a needle. Make a few stitches to join the end of the stem wire to the two free points (Fig 2). Gather the longest side to the point at the end of the fold (Fig 3). Place the free end of the stem wire in the fold and pull the gathering up tight, until you can join the end to the beginning with no stitches showing. This will form a crescent shape (Fig 4). Repeat this process with the two other pieces.

Stem: Join one to the top of a stem wire with binding wire and cover a short length of stem with binding tape. Then fix the other two in the same way, placing them alternately on either side of the stem. Shape the stem so that it echoes the curves in the leaves.

9 Fabric Flower Display

All the little ribbon roses and buds in this Italian jug were cut from one piece of ribbon and the space between them filled with a delicate tracery of dried lady's mantle flowers.

The art of flower arranging is a creative craft and an extremely popular one; if you are not lucky enough to have a source of fresh flowers to constantly draw from, the ability to make some of your own is definitely an asset. Many of the designs which follow will naturally have a predominance of fabric flowers in them, but alone they tend to be rather heavy and stylised and it is an improvement to incorporate the delicate tracery of some other materials, such as feathers and dried plant materials, in your design. The flowers you choose to make should be considered not only for their colour and texture but for their shape. By their method of manufacture a great many artificial flowers are round, so to avoid a vaseful of globular shapes try to choose some varied forms – if not in the flowers themselves then in the accompanying materials. These can be leaves, berries or sprays of flowers. With the vast range of different types of fabrics there are endless varieties which can be assembled. When you are making your choice, apart from the obvious qualities of colour and fabric texture, you should consider a balanced combination of flower shapes. As a general rule for the traditional type of arrangement you will need good round somewhat solid shapes to fill the centre, then some tall thin spikes and some form of profile shape which will lead the eye out from the full centre to the spikes, then finally some leaves to soften the solid mass in the centre. When you come to place them in a vase, do not make all the flowers face forward; some should face sideways as well so that a flower with a good profile, especially the pendulous lily, can be shown to its best advantage.

There are many flowers and leaves for you to select but several controlling factors, apart from the materials you have available, will emerge as you consider contrasts, such as the tonal value of one part to another. Choose dark components for the centres with light edges in the flowers and follow the same formula as a guide to overall arrangements. The quality of texture also deserves consideration. Do not choose too many different varieties for one design – in fact no more than three different types can provide sufficient interest. You may for example choose one type of flower, like the petersham dahlia, and make shiny silk leaves and fur bulrushes to accompany them to create a satisfactory balance. This particular combination is an example of contrast in not only tone and colour, but shape and texture as well within the three types of material used.

There will however be the occasion when you will want to use the same fabric for all your components, so simply choose three different shaped flowers to make. As a general guide always make an uneven number of flowers and vary the size of them slightly if you can. This variation of size can be a definite asset, particularly if you are intending to place a line of flowers through your design. A gradually increasing and decreasing line is much more pleasing than one which comes to an abrupt end.

The little vase of organdie flowers (see Colour Plate) is a typical example of an entire design made with one fabric. The effect is pleasing but to relieve the monotony skeleton magnolia leaves, whose equal delicacy can only enhance the design, are added. Whilst the organdie is white, green beads and sequins are used to match the dyed leaves.

An arrangement of dried plant materials is enriched where a few focal fabric flowers are used. Dried lady's mantle flowers provide a profusion of fluff around the ribbon flowers in the little black and white china jug from Italy. The dried plants you choose to accompany the flowers should not only be a contrast of texture and appearance but should at the same time have some similarity with the type of flowers. This is the case in the basket of cotton poppies where the obvious choice was the ears of barley and the leaves were big and flat like the poppy petals. The seeds in the centres of the hessian flowers seemed similar to those in the dried allium heads; these stand in a large Portuguese wine bottle which is covered with woven rushes, keeping the whole arrangement within the natural shades of brown (see Colour Plate).

Basket of poppies: Baskets and dried materials, being natural, blend happily together. These form an excellent foil for the severe outlines of the wired cotton poppies.

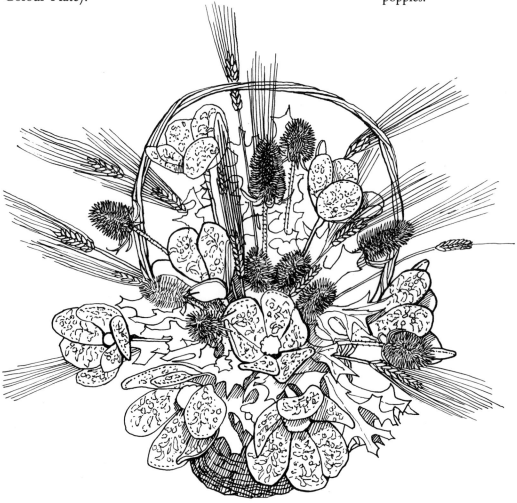

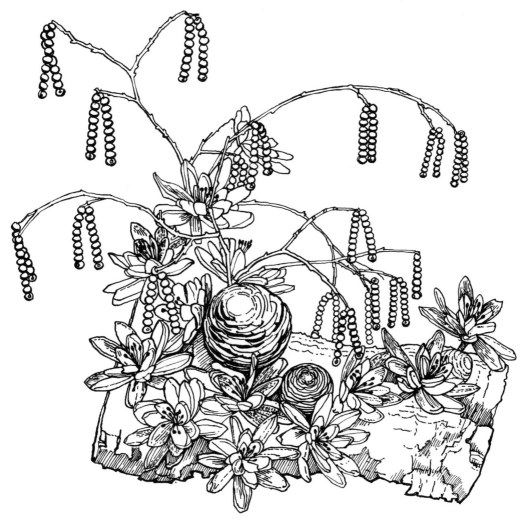

Daisy bank: The colours of these sun daisies are in several shades of mushroom, mossy green and ivory, as it would be a shame to drown the subtle colour of the cork bark. The bead catkins are brown and complete the shape of the whole design.

For an entirely different way of displaying flowers, the piece of cork bark suggests a bank on which daisies would grow. With firm wire stems it was surprisingly easy to push them into the bark. Placed at random as daisies might grow, the height is given to the design with branches of beaded catkins. It is interesting to consider further ways of displaying your flowers in this fashion; use, for example, a flat piece of wood, make many holes in it and plant a selection of flowers and grasses. Standing upright it is possible to see through the stems as one would at the side of a field.

Feathers have a beautiful ethereal quality which, although complete in themselves, makes them one of the best accompaniments to fabric flowers in a vase. Whether they are parts of egret or whole ostrich or peacock feathers, their fluffy texture is a great asset. With the silk roses and lotus seeds, the brightly coloured turkey body feathers filled the surrounding area with constantly moving fluff.

You may have, as I do, a dresser in your dining room with space for a decoration of some kind. In this place, with flowers

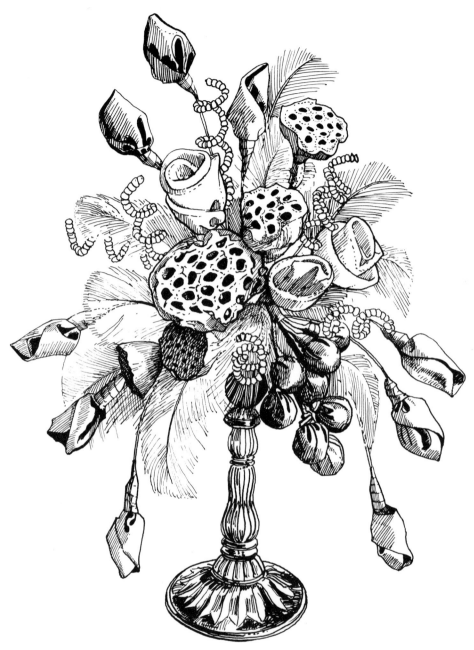

Flowers and feathers in a silver candlestick: This whole arrangement is only 31cm (12in) high. Miniature lotus seeds form the centre around which there are silk roses, bead tendrils and a bunch of grapes. As the materials used are rather dark in tone, turquoise turkey feathers were used to lighten both the colour and the texture.

Christmas table spray: Of
three wired poppies tied with
a velvet ribbon and dried
plant material.

filling many others, an arrangement of fruit and berries seemed
more suitable, illustrated at the opening of Chapter 8. With some
beautiful glass fruit there is an assortment of berries and fruit
made from various fabrics to make an interesting combination
in a pedestal plate. One of the advantages in handmade
flowers is that they obviously do not need water, so a container
is not always necessary. Endless designs can be made where the
wire stems are simply twisted together; it is even possible to find
space for a little tree. Once the combination of flowers and
leaves has been chosen and made, they can be twisted together
into a bunch. At the same time the ends of the wires should be
left free to shape into the roots. The tree must balance naturally,
so if after adjusting the position of the branches it is still un-
steady, simply add extra wires to lengthen the roots.

For an alternative table decoration, a spray of flowers and
leaves can be charming. For Christmas these organdie flowers
have been stitched with gold thread to match their gold bead
centres and fir cones sprayed with gold paint. Together with
holly, the red velvet ribbon completes the traditional festive
colour scheme for the centre of a dining table.

Many houses are designed with combined kitchen and
dining rooms. Even then there may still be an area of wall where
a flower decoration would be acceptable. Silks and satins would
obviously be unsuitable but in the choice of black and white
gingham and black ric-rac, the design blends happily into the
atmosphere of both kitchen and dining areas.

To enter the field of collage and appliqué is outside the
subject of this book, but three-dimensional wallpanels can be
assembled with some of the smaller flowers and berries. An oval
shape is a particularly satisfactory one to contain a floral design
as in the arrangement of assorted dried plant material together
with little silk rose buds and velvet grapes clustered in front of a
woven basketwork plaque which was made in Tuscany (see

Kitchen flowers: These
mob-cap flowers, form the
centre of this spray which,
combined with woolly ball
leonotis, and three big spruce
cones are hung on a wall
of pine panelling, with
glycerined beech leaves.

Colour Plate). In sharp contrast is the strict colour scheme of the Victorian-looking plaque illustrated at the opening of Chapter 4 – cream lace for the flowers and plum-coloured velvet leaves.

Having covered the possibilites of arranging flowers in many unconventional ways, one's mind turns to the area in which fabric flowers were first seen in fashion. One of the most widely accepted areas where fabric flowers occur is in the fashion field. What better use to put your flower making skills than to use remnants of material from dressmaking to make a matching flower. There are special requirements for dress flowers; in particular they must be flat or, if they have any depth, they should be packed full of petals, like the rose or carnation, so that the substance of the flower will not collapse if it is squashed. Remember too that dress flowers in particular come under close scrutiny and so should be the best you can possibly make. Also avoid beads on long wires, because they inevitably get bent and disappear between the petals. I would never use dried plants in the centre either because their stems are too brittle. In view of these limitations we return to the carnation, in which no stamen is visible anyway, or a spray of buds in which the centres are en-

Basket ring: This spray of spring leaves has a little bunch of three lampshade flowers tied with a ribbon in the centre of this basket ring, which was made in Tuscany.

cased. Then you can proudly wear a flower you have made on a dress, coat or hat.

So from dresses to walls, tables to hats, bridal flowers to bouquets, in vases or on coats, the flowers you make can be put in innumerable places. Never feel that your efforts will be fruitless and have no home, and if you find limited time only permits you to make a few flowers, remember that combined with other material you can quickly make an arrangement into which you can display your handsome flowers.

The suggestions given are intended not only as patterns for you to copy direct, but to show that by substituting your own materials and adding your own ideas, the possibilities are enormous. There are exciting prospects ahead of you now in the art of flowermaking.

Acknowledgements

I would like to acknowledge the generous help of the Victoria and Albert Museum, London, The Bath Museum, Mary Thomas's *Dictionary of Embroidery Stitches,* Jacqueline Yorke, Penelope Luxmoore and Pauline Lamb.

List of Materials other than Fabrics

Beads and sequins	Available in many shapes and sizes	Bead shops, eg Ells & Farrer
Binding wire	Available in rolls of various thickness	Florists
Bondina	A double sided iron-on vilene made for hems	Haberdashers
Cherries (artificial)		Florists
Dried flowers and seeds		Florists
Dyes	Fabric hot water dyes	Haberdashers, Hardware
Expanding spring		Hardware
Feathers	Natural feathers	Butchers, Poulterers
	Dyed feathers	In Flower
Flower-making irons	Small iron tools for shaping fabric petals, available singly or in sets	Freeman Bros (Mayfair) Limited
Glue (eg UHU)	Impact plastic glue	Stationers, Ironmongers
Gutta percha	Self-adhesive binding tape	Florists
Iron-on vilene		Haberdashers
Kapok	Cotton waste suitable for stuffings	Haberdashers, Hardware
Milliners' wire	A covered springy wire	Haberdashers
Raffia		Craft shops
Ribbons and trimmings		Haberdashers
Stamens	Ready-made varieties	Craft shops
Stem wires	Stiff florists' wire available in several lengths and weights	Florists
Styrofoam balls	Balls of plastic foam, green or white, in various sizes	Florists
Wire cutters		Hardware

Addresses of the shops mentioned above:
Ells & Farrer, 2 Princes Street, London NW1
Freeman Bros (Mayfair) Ltd, 23/24 Old Bailey, London, EC4M 7EP
In Flower, Yew Tree Cottage, Caundle Marsh, Sherborne, Dorset

Index of Flowers